FUN DIY ARDUINO CIRCUIT PROJECTS

Counting Steps, Produce a QR code, Pressure Sensor, SensorTile.Box, Remote Doorbell, Bottle Filling System, Currency Counter, Hand Gesture Controlled Robotic Arm etc..,

Anbazhagan K

CONTENTS

ACKNOWLEDGMENTS

The writer might want to recognize the diligent work of the article group in assembling this book. He might likewise want to recognize the diligent work of the Raspberry Pi Foundation and the Arduino bunch for assembling items and networks that help to make the Internet of Things increasingly open to the overall population. Yahoo for the democratization of innovation!

INTRODUCTION

The Internet of Things (IOT) is a perplexing idea comprised of numerous PCs and numerous correspondence ways. Some IOT gadgets are associated with the Internet and some are most certainly not. Some IOT gadgets structure swarms that convey among themselves. Some are intended for a solitary reason, while some are increasingly universally useful PCs. This book is intended to demonstrate to you the IOT from the back to front. By structure IOT gadgets, the per user will comprehend the essential ideas and will almost certainly develop utilizing the rudiments to make his or her very own IOT applications. These included ventures will tell the per user the best way to assemble their very own IOT ventures and to develop the models appeared. The significance of Computer Security in IOT gadgets is additionally talked about and different systems for protecting the IOT from unapproved clients or programmers. The most significant takeaway from this book is in structure the tasks yourself.

1. DIY ARDUINO PEDOMETER - COUNTING STEPS UTILIZING ARDUINO AND ACCELEROMETER

Wellness groups are getting extremely famous these days, which considers the strides well as tracks your calories consumed, show heartbeat rate, showtime and some more. What's more, these IoT gadgets are matched up with the cloud so you can without much of a stretch get all the historical backdrop of your physical action on a cell phone. We have likewise manufactured an IoT Based Patient Monitoring System where the basic information have been sent to ThingSpeak to be checked from anyplace.

Pedometers are the gadgets that solitary used to check strides. So in this instructional exercise, we are gonna to assemble a simple and modest DIY Pedometer utilizing Arduino and accelerometer. This Pedometer will tally the quantity of strides and show them on a 16x2 LCD module. This pedometer can be incorporated with this Arduino Smart Watch.

Segments Required

- Arduino Nano

- ADXL 335 Accelerometer

- 16*2 LCD

- LCD I2C Module

- Battery

ADXL335 Accelerometer

The ADXL335 is a finished 3-pivot Analog accelerometer, and it chips away at the rule of capacitive detecting. It is a little, slim, low force module with a polysilicon surface-smaller scale machined sensor and signs molding hardware. ADXL335 accelerometer can gauge the static just as unique increasing speed. Here in this Arduino Pedometer venture, the ADXL335 accelerometer will go about as a Pedometer sensor.

An Accelerometer is a gadget which can change over increasing speed toward any path to its individual variable voltage. This is practiced by utilizing capacitors (allude picture), as the Accel moves, the capacitor present inside it, will likewise experience changes (allude picture) in view of the development, since the capacitance is fluctuated, a variable voltage can likewise be gotten.

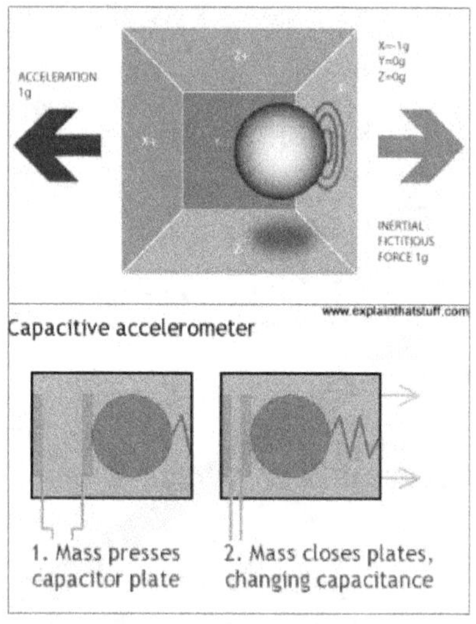

The following are the pictures for Accelerometer from the front and posterior alongside the pin depiction

Pin Description of accelerometer:

- Vcc-5 volt gracefully ought to associate at this pin.

- X-OUT-This pin gives an Analog yield in x heading

- Y-OUT-This pin give an Analog Output in y course

- Z-OUT-This pin gives an Analog Output in z course

- GND-Ground

- ST-This pin utilized for set affectability of sensor

We assemble numerous undertakings utilizing Accelerometer ADXL335 including Gesture controlled robot, Earthquake Detector Alarm, Ping Pong Game, and so on.

Circuit Diagram

Circuit Diagram for Arduino Accelerometer Step Counter is given beneath.

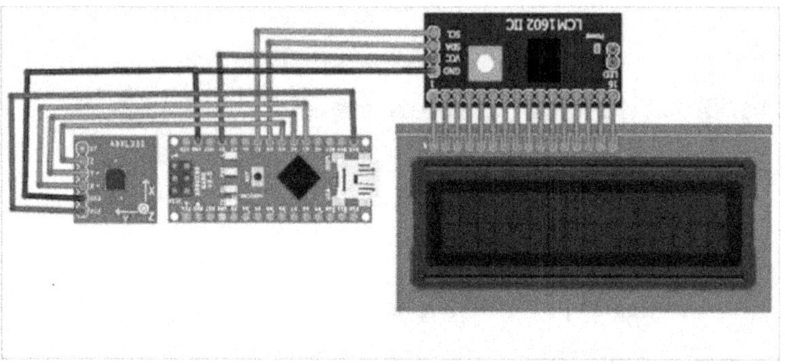

Here, we are interfacing with Arduino Nano with ADXL335 Accelerometer. X, Y, along with Z pins of the accelerometer are associated with Analog pins (A1, A2 along with A3) of Arduino Nano. To interface 16x2 LCD modules with Arduino, we are utilizing the I2C module. SCL and SDA pins of the I2C module are associated with A5 and A4 pins of Arduino Nano, individually. Complete associations are given in the underneath table:

Arduino Nano	ADXL335
3.3V	VCC
GND	GND
A1	X
A2	Y
A3	Z
Arduino Nano	**LCD I2C Module**
5V	VCC
GND	GND
A4	SDA
A5	SCL

We initially assembled this Pedometer utilizing Arduino arrangement on a breadboard

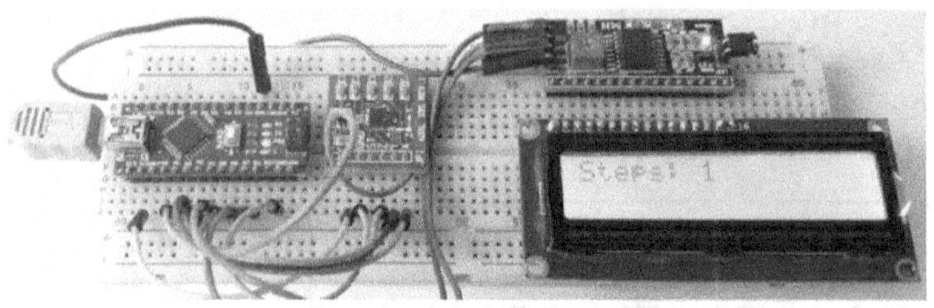

What's more, after fruitful testing we recreated it on Perfboard by fastening all the part on Perfboard as demonstrated as follows:

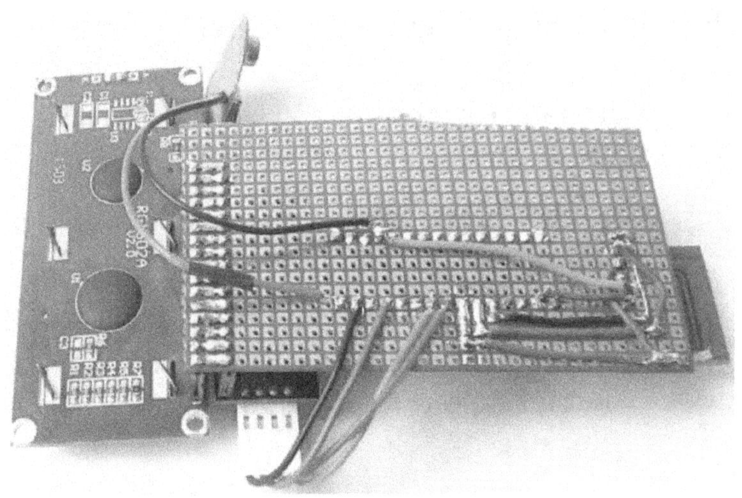

How Pedometer Works?

A pedometer figures the all out no of steps taken by an individual utilizing the three parts of movement that are forward, vertical, and side. The pedometer framework utilizes an accelerometer to get these qualities. Accelerometer constantly refreshes the most extreme and least estimations of the 3-hub speeding up after each characterized no. of tests. The normal estimation of these 3-hub (Max + Min)/2, is known as the dynamic edge level, and this limit esteem is utilized to choose whether the progression is taken or not.

While running, the pedometer can be in any direction, so the pedometer figures the means utilizing the hub whose speeding up change is the biggest.

Presently let me give you a snappy walkthrough of

the working of this Arduino Pedometer:

- Initially the pedometer begins the alignment when it gets controlled.

- In this point in the void circle work, it consistently gets the information from X, Y, along with Z-pivot.

- From that point onward, it computes the absolute speeding up vector from the beginning stage.

- Increasing speed vector is the square root $(x^2+y^2+z^2)$ of the X, Y, and Z-pivot esteems.

- In this point it contrasts the normal increasing speed esteems along with the edge esteems to check the progression number.

- On the off chance that the speeding up vector crosses the edge esteem, at that point it builds the progression tally; else, it disposes of the invalid vibrations.

Programming the Arduino Step Counter

The total Arduino Step Counter Code is given toward the finish of this record. Here we are clarifying some significant scraps of this code.

Not surprisingly, start the code by including all the needed libraries. ADXL335 accelerometer doesn't require any library as it gives a simple yield.

```
#include <LiquidCrystal_I2C.h>
```

From that point onward, characterize the Arduino Pins, where the accelerometer is associated.

```
const int xpin = A1;

const int ypin = A2;

const int zpin = A3;
```

Characterize the limit an incentive for the accelerometer. This edge worth will be contrasted with the quickening vector with compute the quantity of steps.

```
float threshold = 6;
```

Inside the void arrangement, work adjusts the framework when it is fueled.

```
calibrate();
```

Inside the void circle work, it will peruse the X, Y and Z-hub esteems for 100 examples.

```
for (int a = 0; a < 100; a++)

  {

    xaccl[a] = float(analogRead(xpin) - 345);

    delay(1);

    yaccl[a] = float(analogRead(ypin) - 346);

    delay(1);

    zaccl[a] = float(analogRead(zpin) - 416);

    delay(1);
```

In the wake of getting the 3-pivot esteems, figure the all out quickening vector by taking the square base of X, Y, and Z-hub esteems.

```
totvect[a] = sqrt(((xaccl[a] - xavg) * (xaccl[a] - xavg))
+ ((yaccl[a] - yavg) * (yaccl[a] - yavg)) + ((zval[a] -
zavg) * (zval[a] - zavg)));
```

At that point ascertain the normal of the most extreme and least quickening vector esteems.

```
totave[a] = (totvect[a] + totvect[a - 1]) / 2 ;
```

Presently contrast the normal increasing speed and the edge. In case the normal is more prominent than the edge, at that point increment the progression tally and raise the banner.

```
if (totave[a] > threshold && flag == 0)

    {

        steps = steps + 1;

        flag = 1; }
```

On the off chance that the normal is more prominent than the edge however the banner is raised, at that point sit idle.

```
else if (totave[a] > threshold && flag == 1)

    {

        // Don't Count
```

```
}
```

In the event that the all out normal is not as much as limit and banner is raised, at that point put the banner down.

```
if (totave[a] < threshold  && flag == 1)

    {

        flag = 0;

    }
```

Print the quantity of steps on sequential screen and LCD.

```
Serial.println(steps);

lcd.print("Steps: ");

lcd.print(steps);
```

Testing the Arduino Pedometer

When your equipment and code are prepared, associate the Arduino to the PC and transfer the code. Presently take the pedometer arrangement in your grasp and begin strolling bit by bit, it should show the quantity of steps on LCD. In some cases it builds the quantity of steps when pedometer vibrates quickly or gradually.

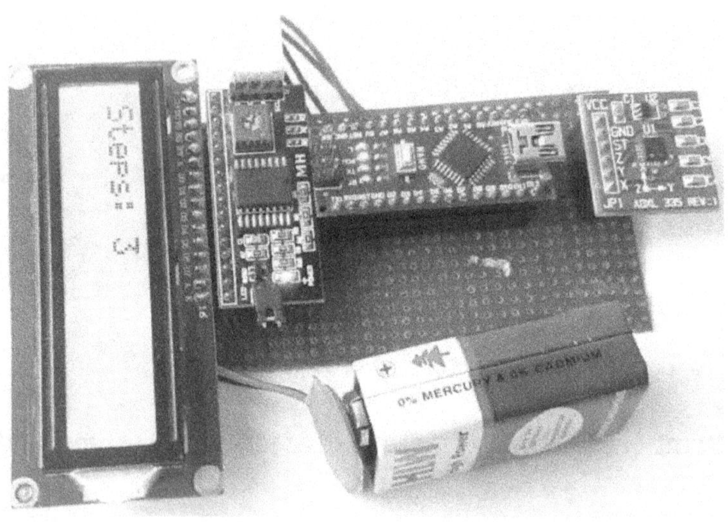

The total code for the ADXL335 pedometer Arduino are given beneath.

Code

```
#include <LiquidCrystal_I2C.h>
LiquidCrystal_I2C lcd(0x27, 16, 2);
const int xpin = A1;
const int ypin = A2;
```

```
const int zpin = A3;
byte p[8] = {
 0x1F,
 0x1F,
 0x1F,
 0x1F,
 0x1F,
 0x1F,
 0x1F,
 0x1F
};
float threshold = 6;
float xval[100] = {0};
float yval[100] = {0};
float zval[100] = {0};
float xavg, yavg, zavg;
int steps, flag = 0;
void setup()
{
 Serial.begin(9600);
 lcd.begin();
 lcd.backlight();
 lcd.clear();
 calibrate();
}
void loop()
{
 for (int w = 0; w < 16; w++) {
  lcd.write(byte(0));
  delay(500);
```

```
}
int acc = 0;
float totvect[100] = {0};
float totave[100] = {0};
float xaccl[100] = {0};
float yaccl[100] = {0};
float zaccl[100] = {0};
for (int a = 0; a < 100; a++)
{
 xaccl[a] = float(analogRead(xpin) - 345);
 delay(1);
 yaccl[a] = float(analogRead(ypin) - 346);
 delay(1);
 zaccl[a] = float(analogRead(zpin) - 416);
 delay(1);
 totvect[a] = sqrt((((xaccl[a] - xavg) * (xaccl[a] - xavg))
+ ((yaccl[a] - yavg) * (yaccl[a] - yavg)) + ((zval[a] - zavg) *
(zval[a] - zavg)));
 totave[a] = (totvect[a] + totvect[a - 1]) / 2 ;
 Serial.println("totave[a]");
 Serial.println(totave[a]);
 delay(100);
 if (totave[a] > threshold && flag == 0)
 {
  steps = steps + 1;
  flag = 1;
 }
 else if (totave[a] > threshold && flag == 1)
 {
  // Don't Count
```

```
    }
    if (totave[a] < threshold  && flag == 1)
    {
      flag = 0;
    }
    if (steps < 0) {
      steps = 0;
    }
    Serial.println('\n');
    Serial.print("steps: ");
    Serial.println(steps);
    lcd.print("Steps: ");
    lcd.print(steps);
    delay(1000);
    lcd.clear();
  }
  delay(1000);
}
void calibrate()
{
  float sum = 0;
  float sum1 = 0;
  float sum2 = 0;
  for (int i = 0; i < 100; i++) {
    xval[i] = float(analogRead(xpin) - 345);
    sum = xval[i] + sum;
  }
  delay(100);
  xavg = sum / 100.0;
  Serial.println(xavg);
```

```
for (int j = 0; j < 100; j++)
{
 yval[j] = float(analogRead(ypin) - 346);
 sum1 = yval[j] + sum1;
}
yavg = sum1 / 100.0;
Serial.println(yavg);
delay(100);
for (int q = 0; q < 100; q++)
{
 zval[q] = float(analogRead(zpin) - 416);
 sum2 = zval[q] + sum2;
}
zavg = sum2 / 100.0;
delay(100);
Serial.println(zavg);
}
```

◆ ◆ ◆

2. PRODUCE A QR CODE UTILIZING ARDUINO AND SHOW IT ON SSD1306 OLED

Arduino QR Code Generator

The "Brisk Response" code or abridged as QR code has become a fundamental piece of our computerized lives, odds are that you're as of now subliminally acquainted with them at this point you've likely been meandering around your nearby supermarket, or perhaps you are perusing your preferred book, or even potentially you are making an online installment with Google Pay, PhonePe or Paytm, or riding the web, and so on. (I guess I could continue endlessly with models huh?) and you had gone over this peculiar looking square thing and thought, what is this square thing in any case and in case you haven't...well, don't stress' will undoubtedly happen at some point or another, so to comprehend the theme better we will do a pleasant little venture with Arduino and

OLED and demystify the accompanying things:

- Essential Concept of the QR code.

- How it functions.

- The most effective method to do your own one of a kind QR code utilizing Arduino.

- Lastly, show it in an OLED (SSD1306) screen.

All in all, What is this QR Code Anyway?

QR code (Quick Response code) is a framework 2D code for perusing information at fast, created by DENSO WAVE in 1994 for the car business of Japan. A QR code packs information productively contrasted with the standard scanner tag, to accomplish this it utilizes four normalized encoding modes (numeric, alphanumeric, byte/paired, and kanji), the innovation was made "open source" for example accessible for everybody along these lines, it picked up prominence quickly. Noteworthy focal points of QR Codes over regular scanner tags are bigger information limit and high adaptation to non-critical failure.

QR code

How QR Code Works?

QR codes (and other information network codes) are intended to be perused by unique apparatuses, not by people, so there's just a particular sum we can comprehend by concentrating outwardly, albeit each code is distinctive in different manners however they contain a couple of fascinating normal highlights QR code we will concentrate some of them

- **Discoverer Patterns:** Large square boxes with a strong box inside in the three corners of the code make it simple to affirm that it's a QR code since there are just three of them, so it's truly clear that where way the code is situated.

- **Arrangement Pattern:** This makes it sure that whatever the direction the code can be decipherable.

- **Timing Pattern:** This runs on a level plane and vertically between the three discoverer designs, utilizing these lines the peruser can decide the size of the code.

- **Variant Information:** There are at present 40 distinct adaptations of the QR code standard, this segment of the code decides the QR code form which is being utilized, for showcasing rendition 1-7 utilized regularly.

- **Configuration Information:** The arrangement accomplices have data about mistake resistance and information covering.

- **Information Area:** This segment of the code contains all the information components and blunder revision code along.

- **Stop Zone:** The dividing in each QR code is obligatory so as to separate the code from its environmental factors.

Different segments of the code are information and excess code.

There are various different highlights and convoluted

points that I won't examine in this instructional exercise, in the event that you do get a kick out of the chance to peruse in more insights concerning the QR code please follow this QR Code instructional exercise by Tan Jin Soon, EPCglobal Singapore Council. Blend Journal, 2008.

The Specification of the QR Code

Symbol Size	Min. 21x21 cell - Max. 177x177 cell (with 4-cells interval)	
Information Type and Volume	Numeric Characters	7,089 characters at maximum
	Alphabets, Signs	4,296 characters at maximum
	Binary (8 bit)	2,953 characters at maximum
	Kanji Characters	1,817 characters at maximum
Conversion efficiency	Numeric Characters Mode	3.3 cells/character
	Alphanumeric/Signs Mode	5.5 cells/character
	Binary (8 bit) Mode	8 cells/character
	Kanji Characters Mode (13 bit)	13 cells/character

Error correction function-ality	Level L	Approx. 7% of the symbol area restored at maximum
	Level M	Approx. 15% of the symbol area restored at maximum
	Level Q	Approx. 25% of the symbol area restored at maximum
	Level H	Approx. 30% of the symbol area restored at maximum
Linking functionality	Possible to be divided into 16 symbols at maximum	

Producing your own one of a kind QR code

Follow the means referenced beneath to produce your own one of a kind QR code, in this model,

To create a QR code go to this site and on the off chance that you take a gander at the top side of the site you can see a rundown of choices, in this instructional exercise we are producing a QR code for a URL, so we are going to

- Snap on the URL tab and glue the URL for the Google in the Enter URL segment.

- Snap on spare.

- Give a document name for the yield record.

- Select PNG as our favored document position.

- what's more, click spare.

The picture beneath will give you an unmistakable thought regarding the procedure

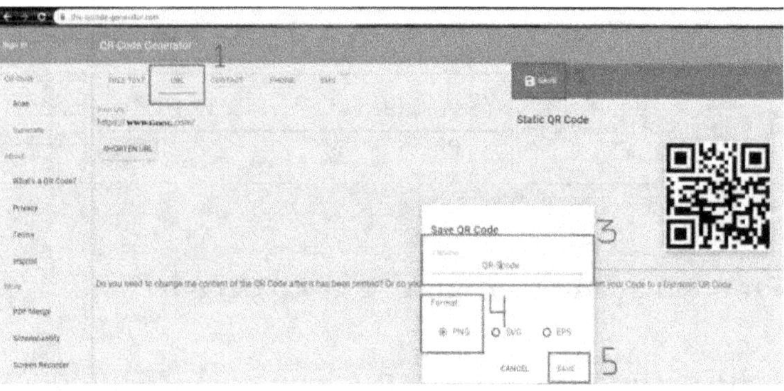

Our dearest microcontroller "Arduino" isn't that shrewd enough that it could simply gather the crude PNG picture and shows it in the OLED show. In this lines, to show the QR code to the OLED we have to follow some straightforward advances and convert the PNG picture to a bitmap cluster meaningful by

Arduino. This change we have recently done while interfacing SSD1306 OLED with Arduino and interfacing Graphical LCD with Arduino. We additionally interfaced SSD1306 OLED with Raspberry Pi, ESP32, NodeMCU, and numerous different microcontrollers. Bitmap cluster change should be possible in beneath two stages:

- Changing over the PNG to BMP design.

- Convert the BMP picture to a variety of HEX codes.

Changing over the PNG to BMP group

To change over the downloaded PNG picture to BMP picture, go to this site along with in the picture converter segment and

- Snap on the dropdown menu and select

- Convert to BMP

- Snap Go

The picture underneath will give you an unmistakable thought regarding the procedure:

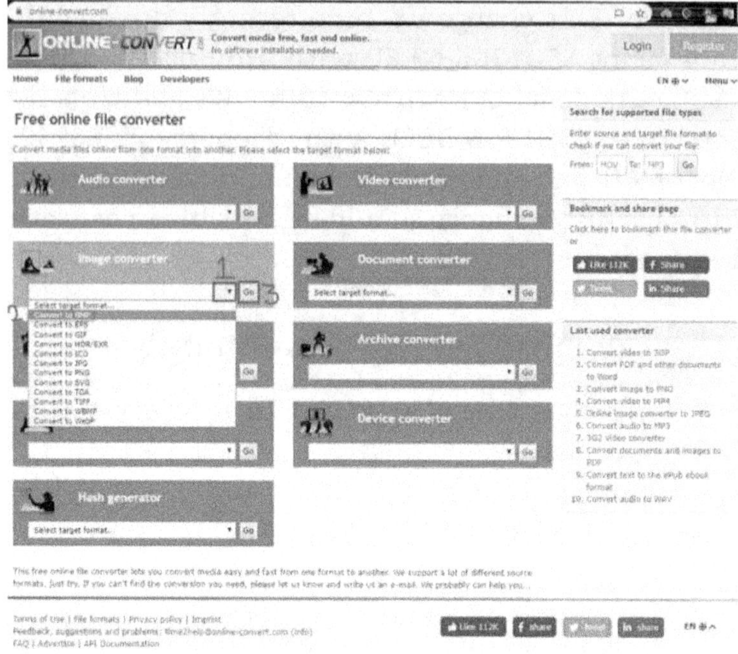

You will be given another page resembles the underneath picture:

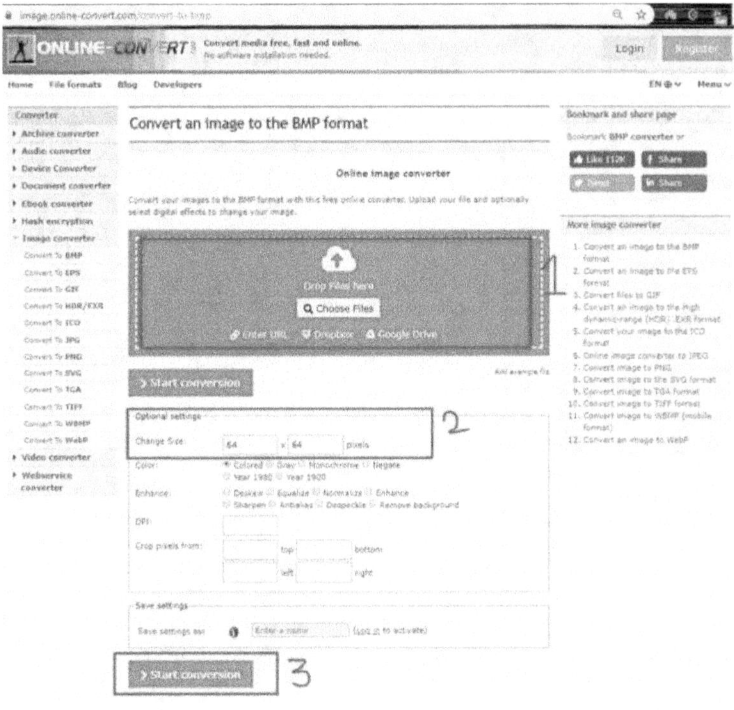

- Snap on the Choose Files tab along with select the downloaded picture

- In the Optional settings, board type your ideal size (we are utilizing a 128x64 OLED)

- Snap on Start change button

You will be given the accompanying page and following a couple of moments your changed over picture will be downloaded if the download doesn't begin consequently tap on the install your document choice:

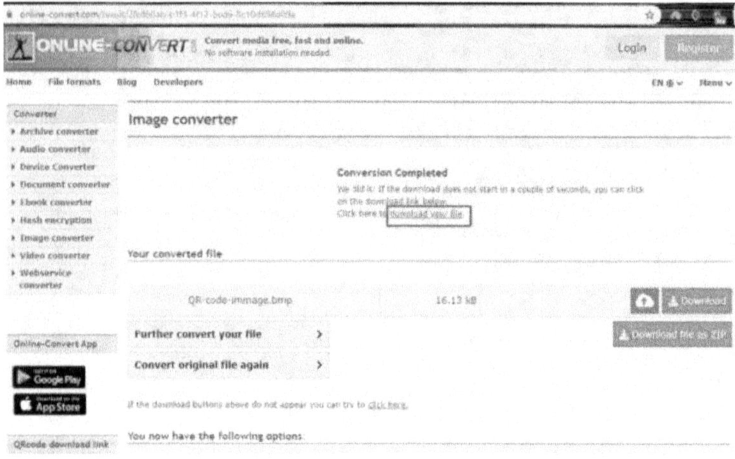

Amazing! Presently we got our BMP document its opportunity to change over it to a variety of HEX codes decipherable by an Arduino.

Convert the BMP picture to a variety of HEX codes

To change over the downloaded BMP picture to a HEX exhibit, go to this site and snap on Tools - > image2cpp

The picture underneath will give you an unmistakable thought regarding the procedure

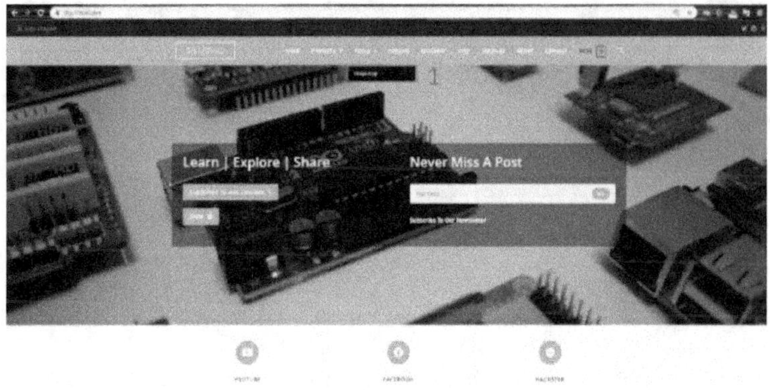

You will be given a screen which has four choices and we will talk about them in subtleties

- Select picture

- Picture Settings

- Review

- Yield

Select picture area

In this area we will choose the picture which we have quite recently changed over to BMP:

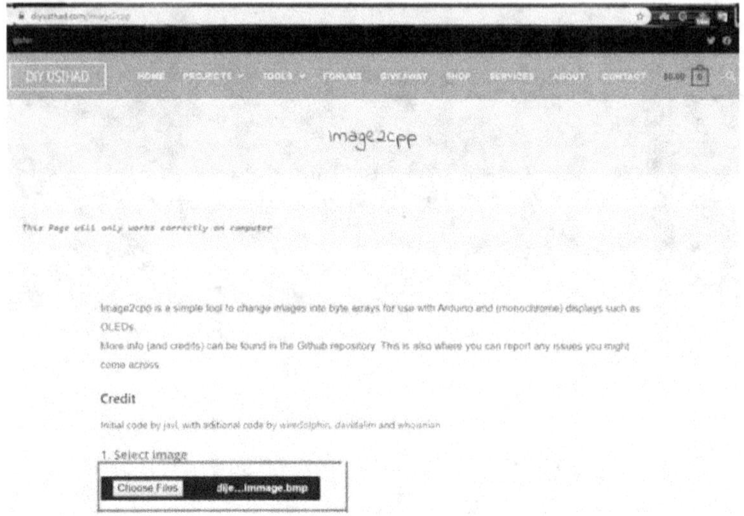

Picture Settings Section

In this area, we will set the canvas size, foundation shading, scaling and focus choices to our necessary worth.

- Canvas size (we set to 128x64 in light of the fact that we are utilizing an OLED with 128x64 pixel thickness).

- In this segment, we can set the foundation shade of the OLED (we pick it to be white).

- Scaling is set to the first size.

- At last, in the middle alternative snap on the even and vertical checkboxes, this will cause the picture to show up in the inside.

The picture underneath will give you an unmistakable thought

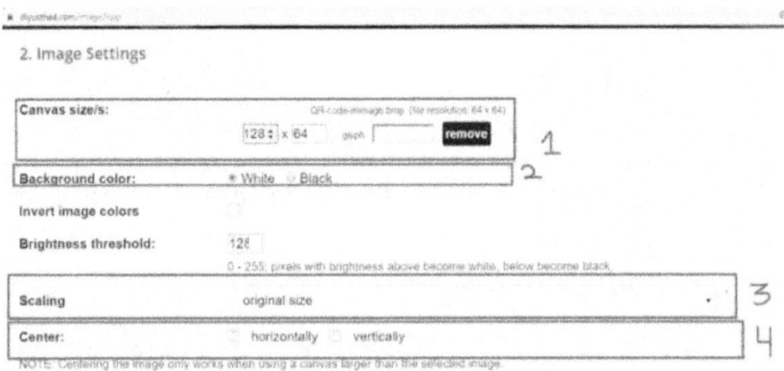

See Section

In the see segment we can see an away from of the picture which will be shown in the OLED like demonstrated as follows:

Yield Section

In the yield area we will produce and duplicate the created code, to do so follow the underneath steps:

- Code yield position (we set it as Arduino code since we are utilizing one).

- Identifier (this alternative sets the name for the produced cluster we leave it default all things considered).

- Draw mode (We set the attract mode alternative to even).

- Lastly, we click on the produce code button this will create the last yield code.

The picture underneath will give you an unmistakable thought

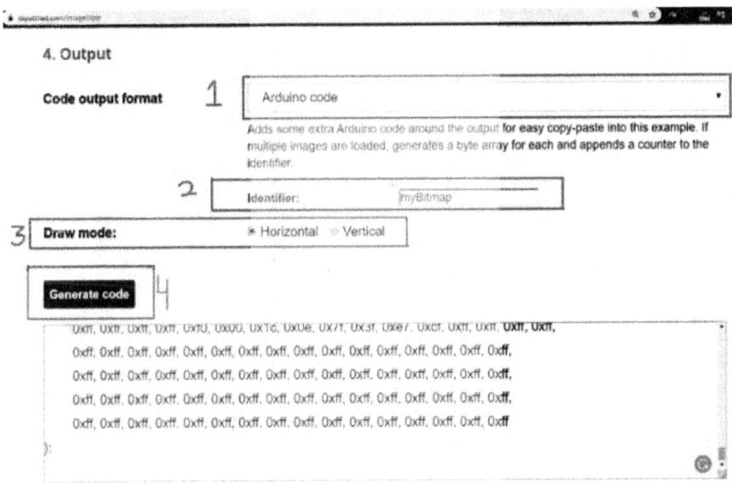

Circuit Diagram

Underneath picture demonstrated the interfacing associations between Arduino Nano and SSD1306:

Arduino Nano Pin	OLED PIN

GND	GND
3.3V	VCC
D13	CLK
D11	MOSI
D8	RES
D9	SDC
D10	CCS

Code Explanation

To show the picture on the OLED we need the assistance of an Arduino library, which can be downloaded from this GitHub vault. Install the U8glib-1.19.1.zip adaptation of the library along with import it in the Arduino IDE. In the event that you are new to Arduino, at that point take the assistance of this connection depicting how to import a library. In the beneath area we will adjust the code to show the recently produced HEX exhibit to the OLED. Complete code is given toward the finish of this article. The Detail Explanation of the code is given beneath.

To begin with, incorporate the downloaded library.

```
#include "U8glib.h" // including the U8glib library
```

At that point characterize all the essential pins for OLED.

```
#define OLED_CLK_PIN 13  //Arduino Digital Pin D13: SCK

#define OLED_MOSI_PIN 11 //Arduino Digital Pin D11: MOSI

#define OLED_RES_PIN 10 //Arduino Digital Pin D10: SS

#define OLED_SDC_PIN 9 //Arduino Digital Pin D9: OC1A

#define OLED_CSS_PIN 8 //Arduino Digital Pin D13: ICP1
```

Instate the u8glib Library.

```
U8GLIB_SH1106_128X64      u8g(OLED_CLK_PIN,
OLED_MOSI_PIN, OLED_RES_PIN, OLED_SDC_PIN,
OLED_CSS_PIN);
```

At that point Include the produced picture exhibit.

```
const uint8_t Helloworld [] PROGMEM = {

  0xff, 0xff, 0xff, 0xff, 0xff, 0xff, 0xff, 0xff, 0xff, 0xff,
0xff, 0xff, 0xff, 0xff, 0xff, 0xff,

  0xff, 0xff, 0xff, 0xff, 0xff, 0xff, 0xff, 0xff, 0xff, 0xff,
0xff, 0xff, 0xff, 0xff, 0xff, 0xff,

  0xff, 0xff, 0xff, 0xff, 0xff, 0xff, 0xff, 0xff, 0xff, 0xff,
0xff, 0xff, 0xff, 0xff,

0xff, 0xff,

  0xff, 0xff, 0xff, 0xff, 0xff, 0xff, 0xff, 0xff, 0xff, 0xff,
0xff, 0xff, 0xff, 0xff, 0xff, 0xff,

  0xff, 0xff, 0xff, 0xff, 0xf0, 0x00, 0x1c, 0x01, 0x87,
0xf0, 0x00, 0x0f, 0xff, 0xff, 0xff, 0xff,

  0xff, 0xff, 0xff, 0xff, 0xf0, 0x00, 0x0c, 0x01, 0x87,
```

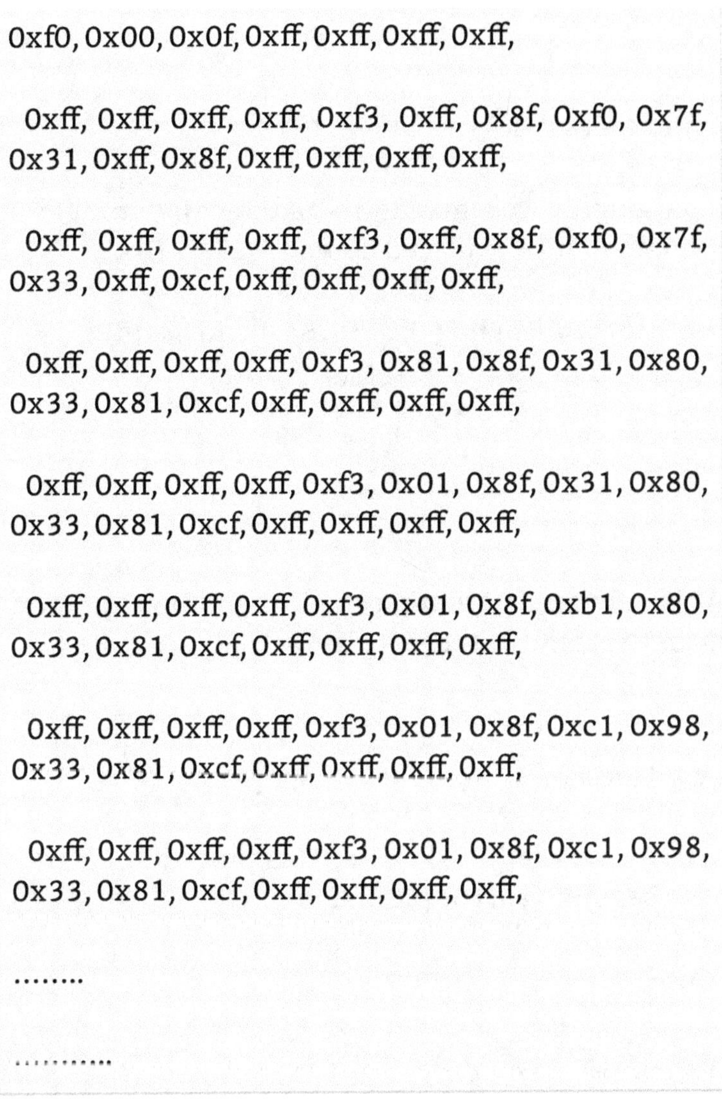

```
0xf0, 0x00, 0x0f, 0xff, 0xff, 0xff, 0xff,

 0xff, 0xff, 0xff, 0xff, 0xf3, 0xff, 0x8f, 0xf0, 0x7f,
0x31, 0xff, 0x8f, 0xff, 0xff, 0xff, 0xff,

 0xff, 0xff, 0xff, 0xff, 0xf3, 0xff, 0x8f, 0xf0, 0x7f,
0x33, 0xff, 0xcf, 0xff, 0xff, 0xff, 0xff,

 0xff, 0xff, 0xff, 0xff, 0xf3, 0x81, 0x8f, 0x31, 0x80,
0x33, 0x81, 0xcf, 0xff, 0xff, 0xff, 0xff,

 0xff, 0xff, 0xff, 0xff, 0xf3, 0x01, 0x8f, 0x31, 0x80,
0x33, 0x81, 0xcf, 0xff, 0xff, 0xff, 0xff,

 0xff, 0xff, 0xff, 0xff, 0xf3, 0x01, 0x8f, 0xb1, 0x80,
0x33, 0x81, 0xcf, 0xff, 0xff, 0xff, 0xff,

 0xff, 0xff, 0xff, 0xff, 0xf3, 0x01, 0x8f, 0xc1, 0x98,
0x33, 0x81, 0xcf, 0xff, 0xff, 0xff, 0xff,

 0xff, 0xff, 0xff, 0xff, 0xf3, 0x01, 0x8f, 0xc1, 0x98,
0x33, 0x81, 0xcf, 0xff, 0xff, 0xff, 0xff,

.........

.............
```

Attract work is utilized to draw the bitmap picture (QR code) on OLED with the assistance of u8g.draw-BitmapP work.

```
void draw(void) {

  // graphic commands to redraw the complete
screen should be placed here

  u8g.drawBitmapP( 0, 0, 16, 64, helloworld);

  .....

  .......
```

At last, in circle() work, call all the important strategies to assemble the picture on OLED

```
void loop() {

  u8g.firstPage();  //A call to this procedure, marks
the beginning of the picture loop.

  do {

    draw();

  } while( u8g.nextPage() ); // A call to this procedure, marks the end of the body of the picture loop.
```

```
  // rebuild the picture after some delay

  delay(1000);

}
```

In the wake of finishing the code, plug in the Arduino in the USB port of your PC, select your COM port and transfer the code. In case you have done everything effectively you will have a working presentation with a QR code on OLED.

I trust you preferred this undertaking and delighted in discovering some new information, continue perusing continue learning and I will see you next time.

Code

```c
/*

    Universal 8bit Graphics Library, http://code.google.com/p/u8glib/

*/

#include "U8glib.h" // including the U8glib library

#define OLED_CLK_PIN 13 //Arduino Digital Pin D13: SCK

#define OLED_MOSI_PIN 11 //Arduino Digital Pin D11: MOSI

#define OLED_RES_PIN 10 //Arduino Digital Pin D10: SS

#define OLED_SDC_PIN 9  //Arduino Digital Pin D9: OC1A

#define OLED_CSS_PIN 8 //Arduino Digital Pin D13: ICP1

U8GLIB_SH1106_128X64        u8g(OLED_CLK_PIN, OLED_MOSI_PIN, OLED_RES_PIN, OLED_SDC_PIN, OLED_CSS_PIN);

/*

    make an object of the U8GLIB_SH1106_128X64 class and initialized the Pins of the arduino

    this method takes five arguments first (SCK_PIN, MOSI_PIN,CS_PIN,A0_pin,RESET_PIN)

*/
```

```
//the custom made Bitmap
const uint8_t Helloworld[] PROGMEM = {
 0xff, 0xff, 0xff, 0xff, 0xff, 0xff, 0xff, 0xff, 0xff, 0xff,
0xff, 0xff, 0xff, 0xff, 0xff, 0xff,

 0xff, 0xff, 0xff, 0xff, 0xff, 0xff, 0xff, 0xff, 0xff, 0xff,
0xff, 0xff, 0xff, 0xff, 0xff, 0xff,

 0xff, 0xff, 0xff, 0xff, 0xff, 0xff, 0xff, 0xff, 0xff, 0xff,
0xff, 0xff, 0xff, 0xff, 0xff, 0xff,

 0xff, 0xff, 0xff, 0xff, 0xff, 0xff, 0xff, 0xff, 0xff, 0xff,
0xff, 0xff, 0xff, 0xff, 0xff, 0xff,

0xff, 0xff, 0xff, 0xff, 0xf3, 0xff, 0x8f, 0xf0, 0x7f, 0x31,
0xff, 0x8f, 0xff, 0xff, 0xff, 0xff,

 0xff, 0xff, 0xff, 0xff, 0xf0, 0x00, 0x1c, 0x01, 0x87,
0xf0, 0x00, 0x0f, 0xff, 0xff, 0xff, 0xff,

 0xff, 0xff, 0xff, 0xff, 0xf0, 0x00, 0x0c, 0x01, 0x87,
0xf0, 0x00, 0x0f, 0xff, 0xff, 0xff, 0xff,

0xff, 0xff, 0xff, 0xff, 0xf3, 0x01, 0x8f, 0xc0, 0x67,
0x33, 0x81, 0xcf, 0xff, 0xff, 0xff, 0xff,

 0xff, 0xff, 0xff, 0xff, 0xf3, 0x3f, 0x8f, 0xf0, 0x7f,
0x33, 0xff, 0xcf, 0xff, 0xff, 0xff, 0xff,

 0xff, 0xff, 0xff, 0xff, 0xf3, 0x81, 0x8f, 0x31, 0x80,
0x33, 0x81, 0xcf, 0xff, 0xff, 0xff, 0xff,

 0xff, 0xff, 0xff, 0xff, 0xf3, 0x01, 0x8f, 0x31, 0x80,
0x33, 0x81, 0xcf, 0xff, 0xff, 0xff, 0xff,

 0xff, 0xff, 0xff, 0xff, 0xf3, 0x01, 0x8f, 0xb1, 0x80,
```

0x33, 0x81, 0xcf, 0xff, 0xff, 0xff, 0xff,

0xff, 0xff, 0xff, 0xff, 0xf3, 0x01, 0x8f, 0xc1, 0x98,
0x33, 0x81, 0xcf, 0xff, 0xff, 0xff, 0xff,

0xff, 0xff, 0xff, 0xff, 0xf3, 0x01, 0x8f, 0xc1, 0x98,
0x33, 0x81, 0xcf, 0xff, 0xff, 0xff, 0xff,

0xff, 0xff, 0xff, 0xff, 0xf3, 0x01, 0x8f, 0xc0, 0x67,
0x33, 0x81, 0xcf, 0xff, 0xff, 0xff, 0xff,

0xff, 0xff, 0xff, 0xff, 0xf3, 0xff, 0x8f, 0x31, 0xe7,
0x33, 0xff, 0xcf, 0xff, 0xff, 0xff, 0xff,

0xff, 0xff, 0xff, 0xff, 0xf0, 0xff, 0x83, 0x3e, 0x00,
0xcc, 0x67, 0xcf, 0xff, 0xff, 0xff, 0xff,

0xff, 0xff, 0xff, 0xff, 0xff, 0x00, 0x7c, 0xff, 0xc3,
0xf1, 0xe0, 0x0f, 0xff, 0xff, 0xff, 0xff,

0xff, 0xff, 0xff, 0xff, 0xff, 0x00, 0x7c, 0xff, 0xe7,
0xf3, 0xe0, 0x0f, 0xff, 0xff, 0xff, 0xff,

0xff, 0xff, 0xff, 0xff, 0xff, 0x00, 0x7c, 0xff, 0xe7,
0xf1, 0xe0, 0x0f, 0xff, 0xff, 0xff, 0xff,

0xff, 0xff, 0xff, 0xff, 0xf0, 0xf9, 0x8f, 0x0e, 0x78,
0xf0, 0x7f, 0xcf, 0xff, 0xff, 0xff, 0xff,

0xff, 0xff, 0xff, 0xff, 0xf0, 0xf9, 0x8f, 0x0e, 0x78,
0xf0, 0x7f, 0xcf, 0xff, 0xff, 0xff, 0xff,

0xff, 0xff, 0xff, 0xff, 0xf3, 0x19, 0xf3, 0xce, 0x18,
0x0f, 0x9e, 0x3f, 0xff, 0xff, 0xff, 0xff,

0xff, 0xff, 0xff, 0xff, 0xf3, 0x19, 0xe3, 0xce, 0x18,
0x0f, 0x9e, 0x3f, 0xff, 0xff, 0xff, 0xff,

0xff, 0xff, 0xff, 0xff, 0xf0, 0x07, 0x83, 0x0f, 0x80,
0xf3, 0x80, 0x0f, 0xff, 0xff, 0xff, 0xff,

0xff, 0xff, 0xff, 0xff, 0xf0, 0x07, 0x83, 0x0f, 0x80,
0xf3, 0x80, 0x0f, 0xff, 0xff, 0xff, 0xff,

0xff, 0xff, 0xff, 0xff, 0xf1, 0xc7, 0xe0, 0xf3, 0xe3,
0x7c, 0x40, 0x8f, 0xff, 0xff, 0xff, 0xff,

0xff, 0xff, 0xff, 0xff, 0xf3, 0xe7, 0xf0, 0xf1, 0xe7,
0x3c, 0x61, 0xcf, 0xff, 0xff, 0xff, 0xff,

0xff, 0xff, 0xff, 0xff, 0xf3, 0xe7, 0xf0, 0xf9, 0xe7,
0x3c, 0x60, 0xcf, 0xff, 0xff, 0xff, 0xff,

0xff, 0xff, 0xff, 0xff, 0xf3, 0xff, 0x8f, 0x31, 0xe7,
0x33, 0xff, 0xcf, 0xff, 0xff, 0xff, 0xff,

0xff, 0xff, 0xff, 0xff, 0xf0, 0x00, 0x0c, 0xce, 0x67,
0x30, 0x00, 0x0f, 0xff, 0xff, 0xff, 0xff,

0xff, 0xff, 0xff, 0xff, 0xf0, 0x00, 0x0c, 0xce, 0x67,
0x30, 0x00, 0x0f, 0xff, 0xff, 0xff, 0xff,

0xff, 0xff, 0xff, 0xff, 0xf8, 0x00, 0x1c, 0x4e, 0x27,
0x38, 0x00, 0x1f, 0xff, 0xff, 0xff, 0xff,

0xff, 0xff, 0xff, 0xff, 0xff, 0xff, 0xfc, 0x3e, 0x1f, 0x3f,
0xff, 0xff, 0xff, 0xff, 0xff, 0xff,

0xff, 0xff, 0xff, 0xff, 0xff, 0xff, 0xfc, 0x3e, 0x1e, 0x3f,
0xff, 0xff, 0xff, 0xff, 0xff, 0xff,

0xff, 0xff, 0xff, 0xff, 0xf0, 0xe1, 0x8f, 0x3e, 0x60,
0x33, 0xff, 0xcf, 0xff, 0xff, 0xff, 0xff,

0xff, 0xff, 0xff, 0xff, 0xf0, 0xe1, 0x8f, 0x3e, 0x60,

0x33, 0xff, 0xcf, 0xff, 0xff, 0xff, 0xff,

0xff, 0xff, 0xff, 0xff, 0xff, 0x19, 0xf0, 0xcf, 0xf8, 0xfc,
0x00, 0x3f, 0xff, 0xff, 0xff, 0xff,

0xff, 0xff, 0xff, 0xff, 0xf3, 0x01, 0x8c, 0xf1, 0xe0,
0x03, 0xfe, 0x0f, 0xff, 0xff, 0xff, 0xff,

0xff, 0xff, 0xff, 0xff, 0xf3, 0x01, 0x8f, 0xc1, 0x83,
0xcf, 0x80, 0x0f, 0xff, 0xff, 0xff, 0xff,

0xff, 0xff, 0xff, 0xff, 0xf3, 0x01, 0x8f, 0xc1, 0x87,
0xcf, 0x80, 0x0f, 0xff, 0xff, 0xff, 0xff,

0xff, 0xff, 0xff, 0xff, 0xf3, 0xff, 0x8c, 0xff, 0xe1, 0xc0,
0x18, 0x0f, 0xff, 0xff, 0xff, 0xff,

0xff, 0xff, 0xff, 0xff, 0xf3, 0xff, 0x8c, 0xff, 0xe0, 0xc0,
0x18, 0x0f, 0xff, 0xff, 0xff, 0xff,

0xff, 0xff, 0xff, 0xff, 0xf1, 0xff, 0x8c, 0xff, 0xf0, 0xc0,
0x18, 0x0f, 0xff, 0xff, 0xff, 0xff,

0xff, 0xff, 0xff, 0xff, 0xf0, 0x00, 0x0c, 0x0e, 0x7f,
0x3f, 0xe7, 0xcf, 0xff, 0xff, 0xff, 0xff,

0xff, 0xff, 0xff, 0xff, 0xf0, 0x00, 0x1c, 0x0e, 0x7f,
0x3f, 0xe7, 0xcf, 0xff, 0xff, 0xff, 0xff,

0xff, 0xff, 0xff, 0xff, 0xff, 0xff, 0xff, 0xff, 0xff, 0xff,
0xff, 0xff, 0xff, 0xff, 0xff, 0xff,

0xff, 0xff, 0xff, 0xff, 0xff, 0xff, 0xff, 0xff, 0xff, 0xff,
0xff, 0xff, 0xff, 0xff, 0xff, 0xff,

0xff, 0xff, 0xff, 0xff, 0xff, 0xff, 0xff, 0xff, 0xff, 0xff,
0xff, 0xff, 0xff, 0xff, 0xff, 0xff,

0xff, 0xff, 0xff, 0xff, 0xff, 0xff, 0xff, 0xff, 0xff, 0xff,
0xff, 0xff, 0xff, 0xff, 0xff, 0xff

0xff, 0xff, 0xff, 0xff, 0xff, 0x19, 0xf0, 0xcf, 0xf8, 0xfc,
0x00, 0x3f, 0xff, 0xff, 0xff, 0xff,

0xff, 0xff, 0xff, 0xff, 0xf0, 0xff, 0x83, 0x3e, 0x00,
0xcc, 0x67, 0xcf, 0xff, 0xff, 0xff, 0xff,

0xff, 0xff, 0xff, 0xff, 0xf3, 0x19, 0x8c, 0x3e, 0x07,
0x00, 0x18, 0x3f, 0xff, 0xff, 0xff, 0xff,

0xff, 0xff, 0xff, 0xff, 0xf3, 0x39, 0x9c, 0x3e, 0x07,
0x00, 0x18, 0x3f, 0xff, 0xff, 0xff, 0xff,

0xff, 0xff, 0xff, 0xff, 0xff, 0xff, 0xfc, 0x3e, 0x1f, 0x3f,
0x98, 0x3f, 0xff, 0xff, 0xff, 0xff,

0xff, 0xff, 0xff, 0xff, 0xff, 0xff, 0xfc, 0x3e, 0x1f, 0x3f,
0x98, 0x3f, 0xff, 0xff, 0xff, 0xff,

0xff, 0xff, 0xff, 0xff, 0xf0, 0x00, 0x1f, 0x01, 0xff,
0x33, 0x9f, 0xcf, 0xff, 0xff, 0xff, 0xff,

0xff, 0xff, 0xff, 0xff, 0xf0, 0x00, 0x0f, 0x01, 0xff,
0x33, 0x9f, 0xcf, 0xff, 0xff, 0xff, 0xff,

0xff, 0xff, 0xff, 0xff, 0xf1, 0xff, 0x8f, 0xc7, 0x80,
0x3f, 0x9f, 0xff, 0xff, 0xff, 0xff, 0xff,

0xff, 0xff, 0xff, 0xff, 0xf3, 0xff, 0x8f, 0xcf, 0x80, 0x3f,
0x9f, 0xff, 0xff, 0xff, 0xff, 0xff,

0xff, 0xff, 0xff, 0xff, 0xf3, 0xff, 0x8f, 0xcf, 0x80, 0x3f,
0x1f, 0xff, 0xff, 0xff, 0xff, 0xff,

0xff, 0xff, 0xff, 0xff, 0xf3, 0x01, 0x8c, 0x30, 0x60,

```
0x00, 0x1f, 0xff, 0xff, 0xff, 0xff, 0xff,

  0xff, 0xff, 0xff, 0xff, 0xf3, 0x01, 0x8c, 0x30, 0x60,
0x00, 0x1f, 0xff, 0xff, 0xff, 0xff, 0xff,

  0xff, 0xff, 0xff, 0xff, 0xf3, 0x01, 0x8c, 0xf1, 0xe0,
0x03, 0xfe, 0x0f, 0xff, 0xff, 0xff, 0xff,

};

void draw(void) {

  // graphic commands to redraw the complete screen
  should be placed here

  u8g.drawBitmapP( 0, 0, 16, 64, Helloworld);

  /*

    drawBitmapP Method takes five arguments

    First: X-position (left position of the bitmap).

    Secound: Y-position (upper position of the bitmap).

    Third: Number of bytes of the bitmap in horizontal
  direction. The width of the bitmap is cnt/8.

    Fourth: Height of the bitmap.

    Fifth: Bitmap array.

  */

  /*

    Draw a bitmap at the specified x/y position (upper
  left corner of the bitmap).

    Parts of the bitmap may be outside the display
```

boundaries.The bitmap is specified by the array bitmap.

A cleared bit means: Do not draw a pixel.

A set bit inside the array means: Write pixel with the current color index.For a monochrome display,

the color index 0 will usually clear a pixel and the color index 1 will set a pixel.

```
*/
}
void setup() {
  // empty setup function as the library manages all internally
}
void loop() {
  u8g.firstPage(); //A call to this procedure, marks the beginning of the picture loop.
  do {
    draw();
  } while( u8g.nextPage() ); // A call to this procedure, marks the end of the body of the picture loop.
  // rebuild the picture after some delay
  delay(1000);
}
```

3. THE MOST EFFECTIVE METHOD TO INTERFACE BMP280 PRESSURE SENSOR MODULE WITH ARDUINO

In the event that you need to manufacture your own temperature checking framework or to quantify the elevation of your automaton or basically need to gauge the barometrical weight in your general vicinity, at that point outstanding amongst other module for you to use in your task is the BMP280 Pressure sensor module. BMP280 is supreme weight and temperature observing sensor which is the redesigned form of

BMP085, BMP180, BMP183 sensors. For what reason is it called a redesigned form? It will be talked about in the accompanying areas. We have just utilized the more established form BMP180 with Arduino in one of our past instructional exercises.

BMP280 sensor module can be utilized alongside microcontrollers like Arduino, PIC, AVR, and so forth. For this task we are gonna to utilize Arduino Uno with BMP280 alongside a LCD 16x2 presentation module, to show estimations of temperature and weight. Before interfacing the BMP280 with Arduino, we have to install the BMP280 Arduino library, which is created by Adafruit. Snap on this Adafruit BMP280 library connect to open the individual Github page and add the header document to your Arduino IDE.

Parts Required

- Arduino

- BMP280

- Interfacing Wires

- Bread Board

- LCD-16x2

BMP280 Pressure Sensor Module:

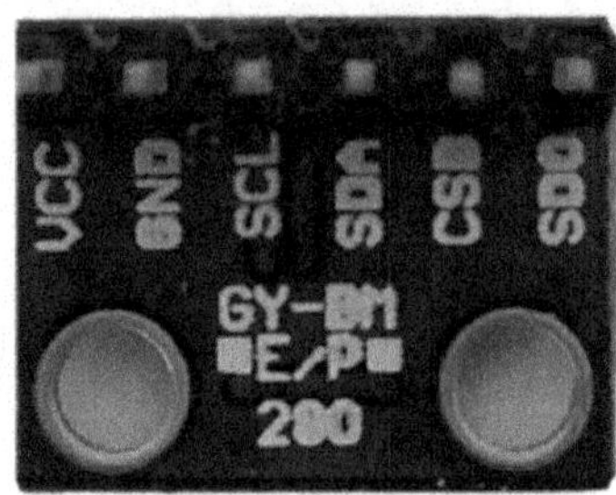

The BMP280 sensor module works with the base voltage (VDD) of 1.71V, though the past adaptation sensor modules take a shot at 1.8V (VDD). With regards to current utilization BMP280 devours 2.7uA, while the BMP180 expends 12uA, and BMP183 and BMP085 expend 5uA each. The BMP280 additionally bolsters new channel modes. The BMP280 sensor module underpins I2c, and SPI conventions, though the rest of the sensor bolsters either I2c or SPI. The BMP280 sensor module has an exactness of ±0.12 hPa, which is proportionate to ±1 m distinction in elevation. Because of these key highlights, it is for the most part utilized in different applications. The BMP sensor comprises of a Pressure detecting component, Humidity detecting component and Temperature detecting component which are additionally associated with Pressure front-end, Humidity front-end, and temperature front-end. These front end IC's are affectability simple intensifiers that are utilized in the enhancement of little signals. The yield of this simple front-end IC's is taken care of to ADC as an information signal. In this the simple qualities are changed over to advanced voltage and this voltage is taken care of to the rationale circuits for additional interface with the outside world.

The BMP280 sensor module comprises of three force modes rest mode, constrained mode, and Normal Mode. In rest mode, no estimations are performed and power utilization is at the very least. In constrained mode, a solitary estimation is performed by the chose estimation and channel choices. Ordinary mode consistently cycles among estimation and reserve period, and the cycles timeframe will be characterized by Tstandby. The current in the backup mode is somewhat higher than the rest mode.

Circuit graph to interface BMP280 with Arduino:

The circuit graph to associate the Arduino with the BMP280 sensor and the LCD is demonstrated as follows. On the off chance that you are totally new to Arduino and LCD, at that point you can check this Arduino LCD instructional exercise to see how to utilize Arduino with LCD shows.

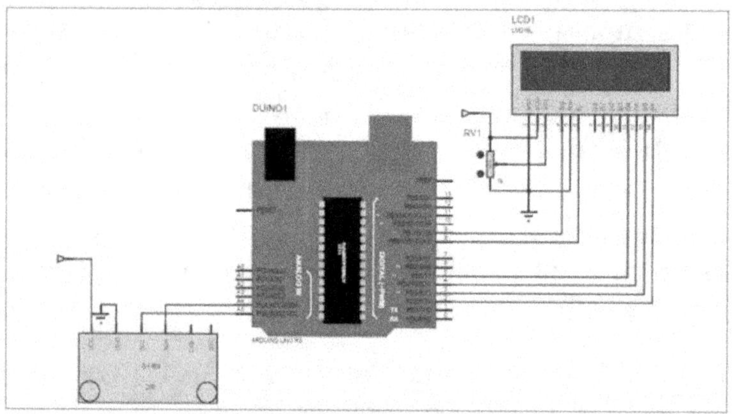

The VCC along with GND pins of the sensor are associated with the 3v3 along with GND pins of the Arduino. The SCL and SDA pins of the sensor are associated with the A5 and A4 of the Arduino board. The LCD associations are as per the following

LCD Pin Name	Arduino Pin
VSS and RW	GND

RS	D9
E	D8
D4, D5, D6, D7	D5,D4,D3,D2

Arduino Program to Interface BMP280 with Arduino:

The total BMP280 Arduino code can be found at the base of this page which can be transferred legitimately to your Arduino board. The clarification of the equivalent is given beneath

These libraries are incorporated for empowering the unique capacities. The #include <Adafruit_BMP280.h> header records we can legitimately peruse the qualities originating from the sensor. The #include <Wire.h> header is useful in utilizing I2C correspondence. The #include <LiquidCrystal.h> header is utilized to get to the exceptional capacity of LCD like lcd.print(), Lcd.setCursor(), along with etc these header documents can be installed utilizing the connection which is given previously. The installed document will be in zip group. Presently open Arduino select Sketch>include library>Add.zip library. Presently include the downloaded record.

```
#include <Wire.h>

#include <SPI.h>

#include <Adafruit_BMP280.h>

#include <LiquidCrystal.h>
```

Making on object BMP for Adafruit_BMP280. An item record is made to get to extraordinary capacities.

```
Adafruit_BMP280 bmp; // I2C
```

Setting the pins of the Arduino to speak with the LCD. Utilizing these pins information will be moved.

```
LiquidCrystal LCD(9, 8, 5, 4, 3, 2);
```

Instating the LCD and Serial Communication.

```
void setup() {

  lcd.begin(16,2);
```

```
  Serial.begin(9600);

  Serial.println(F("BMP280 test"));

  lcd.print("Welcome to ");

  lcd.setCursor(0,1);

  lcd.print("HELLO WORLD");

  delay(1000);

  lcd.clear();

  if (!bmp.begin()) {

    Serial.println(F("Could not find a valid BMP280
sensor, check the wiring!"));

    while (1);

  }
```

This capacity works when the instating of the bmp object is fizzled.

```
  /* Default settings from datasheet. */
```

```
  bmp.setSampling(Adafruit_BMP280::MODE_NOR-
MAL,   /* Operating Mode. */

          Adafruit_BMP280::SAMPLING_X2,     /*
Temp. oversampling */

          Adafruit_BMP280::SAMPLING_X16,    /*
Pressure oversampling */

          Adafruit_BMP280::FILTER_X16,    /* Fil-
tering. */

          Adafruit_BMP280::STAND-
BY_MS_500); /* Standby time. */

}
```

?This part of the code prints the temperature on sequential screen and is for investigating purposes.

```
void loop() {

  Serial.print(F("Temperature = "));

  Serial.print(bmp.readTemperature());

  Serial.println(" *C");
```

The capacity bmp.readPressure and bmp.readTemprature are utilized to conjure uncommon capacities and return the temperature along with weight esteems.

```
lcd.print(bmp.readTemperature());

lcd.print(bmp.readPressure());
```

Working of Arduino BMP280 Pressure Sensor Interfacing Project

The capacities bmp.readTemprature() and bmp.readPressure() are utilized to restore the temperature along with weight esteems. These capacities are a gathering of explanations which play out an exceptional errand, for our situation to return temperature along with weight records. These capacities are summoned utilizing bmp.readTemprature() and bmp.readPressure() capacities. The lcd.setCursor sets the cursor of the LCD to the necessary situation on the screen. The lcd.print order prints the information from the position set by the developer. On the off chance that there is no position set for the LCD of course it takes (0,0) as the underlying position, and nonstop printing the information. The following information takes the situation of the following section, and the method proceeds until it arrives at the finish of the column and movements to the following line.

The BMP280 can be is utilized in Flying toys, cell phones, tablets, PCs, GPS gadgets, Portable medicinal services gadgets, home climate stations, along with etc. By following this technique and utilizing header records and some uncommon capacities, we can without much of a stretch interface BMP280 with the Arduino. Expectation you delighted in this BMP280 Arduino instructional exercise and got the hang of something helpful.

Code

```cpp
#include <Wire.h>
#include <SPI.h>
#include <Adafruit_BMP280.h>
#include <LiquidCrystal.h>
Adafruit_BMP280 bmp; // I2C
//Adafruit_BMP280 bmp(BMP_CS); // hardware SPI
//Adafruit_BMP280 bmp(BMP_CS, BMP_MOSI, BMP_MISO, BMP_SCK);
LiquidCrystal lcd(9, 8, 5, 4, 3, 2);
void setup() {
 lcd.begin(16,2);
 Serial.begin(9600);
 Serial.println(F("BMP280 test"));
 lcd.print("Welcome to ");
 lcd.setCursor(0,1);
 lcd.print("HELLO WORLD");
 delay(1000);
 lcd.clear();
 if (!bmp.begin()) {
  Serial.println(F("Could not find a valid BMP280 sensor, check wiring!"));
  while (1);
 }
 /* Default settings from datasheet. */
  bmp.setSampling(Adafruit_BMP280::MODE_NORMAL,   /* Operating Mode. */
        Adafruit_BMP280::SAMPLING_X2,   /* Temp.
```

```
oversampling */
        Adafruit_BMP280::SAMPLING_X16,   /* Pressure oversampling */
        Adafruit_BMP280::FILTER_X16,    /* Filtering. */
        Adafruit_BMP280::STANDBY_MS_500); /* Standby time. */
}
void loop() {
  Serial.print(F("Temperature = "));
  Serial.print(bmp.readTemperature());
  Serial.println(" *C");
  lcd.setCursor(0,0);
  lcd.print("Temp= ");
  lcd.print(bmp.readTemperature());

  Serial.print(F("Pressure = "));
  Serial.print(bmp.readPressure());
  Serial.println(" Pa");
  lcd.setCursor(0,1);
  lcd.print("Press= ");
  lcd.print(bmp.readPressure());
  Serial.print(F("Approx altitude = "));
  Serial.print(bmp.readAltitude(1018)); /* Adjusted to local forecast! */
  Serial.println(" m");
  Serial.println();
  delay(2000);
}
```

4.
SENSORTILE.BOX REVIEW – TEST AND VALIDATE YOUR WEARABLE IDEAS INSTANTAN-EOUSLY

A couple of years back, if somebody somehow happened to reveal to me a watch couldn't just read a clock yet can likewise gauge the pulse and track calories, I would be overwhelmed by it. Today in excess of a million people, including me own a wearable wellness tracker and it is guage that the market for wearable gadgets would reach $57,653 millions by 2022. From savvy glasses to Diabetes checking gadgets to resource trackers the wearable business is attempting an assortment of items to catch the market. In this lines, in case you have a wearable item thought and is searching for an approach to approve and test it, in this point you may be fortunate in light in case here we will survey the Sensor-Tile.Box (STEVAL-MKSBOX1V1) from STMicroelectronics which can help you too effectively and rapidly approve your remote IoT and wearable gadget thoughts. In case you lean toward recordings over perusing.

Sensor Tile Box – Hardware Overview

The SesnorTile Box here is stuffed in with a great deal of sensors and a Bluetooth module that promptly speaks with a Smartphone application permitting you to manufacture your custom applications as required by your application. The total advancement board comes inside this blue box and we likewise have an extra mounting case on the off chance that we ever need it.

This advancement board has essentially all that you would need to fabricate your wearable and remote IoT applications. It has a Ultra-Low-Power ARM Cortex M4 Microcontroller, Bluetooth 4.2 remote module for BLE correspondence, a Temperature sensor, 6-pivot Inertial Measurement Unit, two 3-Axis accelerometers, one is a ultra-low-power MEMS sensor and other is a high-goals sensor with low commotion. At that point we have a Magnetic sensor, a weight sensor, a sound sensor for example a mouthpiece and a Humidity sensor. On this, the module likewise has its own RTC module, a lithium polymer battery and a SD card inside this blue box to assist you with beginning prototyping out of the crate. The data of sensors in SensorTile box, with their name and highlights, are recorded in the table beneath.

Part Name	Part Number	Features
Microcontroller	STM32L4R9	<ul><li>Ultra-Low Power ARM Cortex-M4</li><li>120MHz with 2048 Kbytes Flash</li><li>DSP and FPU Support</li><li>USB OTG, DFSDM, LCD-TFT, MIPI DSI</li></ul>
Bluetooth v4.2	SPBTLE-1S	<ul><li>Embedded BLE Stack</li></ul>

		<ul><li>Very Low Power BT Module</li><li>Integrated Antenna and Oscillators</li><li>BLE certified / BQE qualified</li></ul>
Temperature Sensor	STTS751	<ul><li>Voltage: 2.25V to 3.6V</li><li>Range: -40°C to 125°C</li><li>Accuracy: ±0.5°C</li><li>Standby current: 3uA</li></ul>
6-Axis IMU Sensor	LM6DSOX	<ul><li>Power Consumption: 0.55mA</li><li>3D Digital Accelerometer</li><li>3D Digital Gyroscope</li><li>Interface: SPI/IIC/ MIPI I3C</li></ul>
3-Axis Accelerometer	LIS2DW12	<ul><li>Ultra-Low Power MEMS sensor</li><li>50nA in Power-down mode</li><li>1uA in low-power mode</li><li>Interface: SPI/IIC</li></ul>
3-Axis Accelerometer	LIS3DHH	<ul><li>Ultra-High Resolution</li><li>±2.5 g full-scale</li><li>Ultra-Low noise: 45 ug/Hz</li><li>Interface: SPI 4-wire</li></ul>
Magnetic Sensor	LIS2MDL	<ul><li>Ultra-Low Power</li><li>Voltage: 1.71V to 3.6V</li><li>Range: ±50 Gauss</li></ul>

		■ Interface: SPI / IIC
Pressure Sensor	LIS2MDL	■ Ultra-Low Power ■ Voltage: 1.71V to 3.6V ■ Range: ±50 Gauss ■ Interface: SPI / IIC
Audio Sensor	MP23ABS1	■ Low Power Microphone ■ With Capacitive Sensing Element ■ Voltage: 1.52V to 3.6V ■ Power: 150 uA max
Humidity Sensor	HTS221	■ Voltage: 1.7V to 3.6V ■ Power: 2uA @ 1Hz ■ Range: 0% to 100% ■ Accuracy: ±3.5%

Investigating the crate, we can see that it has a small scale USB port for charging and correspondence purposes and three LEDs which are BLUE, RED and GREEN. Presently how about we unscrew this crate and investigate what is inside.

As told before you will discover a lithium polymer battery along with our improvement module. Under the battery, we have our SD card space with a 8GB card kingstane card inside it. And afterward we have three press fastens here, a force button, a boot button, and a client configurable catch. At that point we additionally have pinouts of JTAG here. At that point in the event that we pop the board out and turn in around.

We can discover our ARM cortex Microcontroller, Bluetooth Module and the various sensors that I referenced before. Presently as a matter of course, your Lipo battery would have not been associated with your module. So you need to interface your battery terminals to this opening here. At the point when that is done pack your module once more into the blue box and we are good to go.

Sensor Tile Box – Software Overview

Beginning with this board is extremely simple. We have three alternatives here. The initial two alternatives are by utilizing the "ST BLE sensor" Smartphone application created by STMicroelectronics which can be downloaded for both Android and Apple telephones. It has numerous pre-recorded applications that you can dispatch on a solitary snap to perceive how your sensors react.

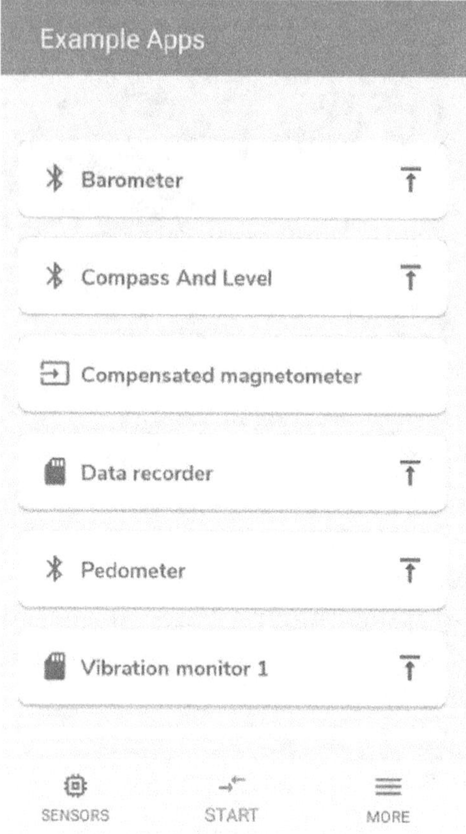

The application likewise has an Expert mode that permits you to do your own custom applications and dispatch it straightforwardly from your telephone. The third choice is to go completely genius by interfacing the board to a STM32 software engineer and programming it utilizing the open advancement condition. For audit, reason lets introduce the "ST BLE sensor" application on my cell phone and check what we can do with it.

Beginning with Sensor Tile Box

At the point when you power the sensor tile box just because you may see the red LED flickering to show the battery is charging. While that is occurring lets download and dispatch the "ST BLE Sensor" application on our cell phone, at that point click on "Interface with a gadget" and you should discover our tilebox there. Snap on it and hold up till your board is associated. You will likewise see the blue LED blazing at regular intervals to show a functioning Bluetooth association. When associated your model application should as of now read and show Temperature, dampness and weight esteems from our sensortile box

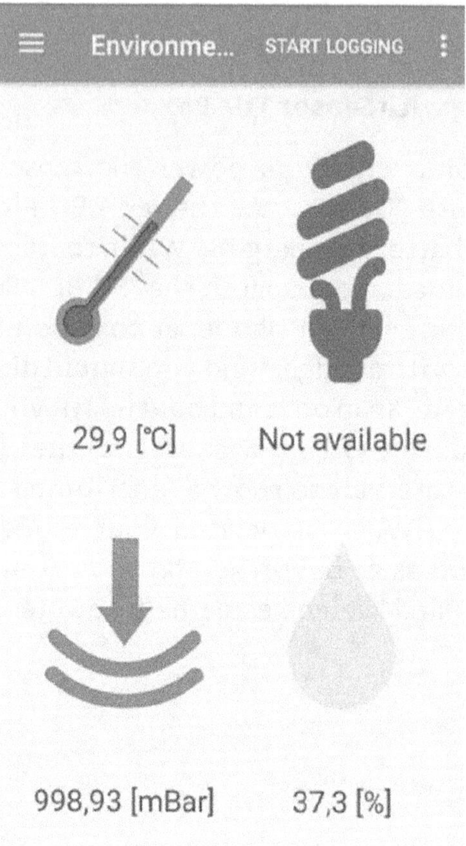

This is only one model program and the application has significantly more for us. To attempt an alternate application Just return to the primary screen and snap on "make new application". Here you will discover all the model applications for your sensor tile box, how about we attempt the sensor combination application for this survey reason. Ringing on the model application will give you a short depiction of the application and you simply need to tap on the "play" catch to transfer the code to your sensor tile box. At that point combine with your case again and your new application will dispatch.

Fun right!! After you are finished playing with all the model applications you can likewise make your own application for SensotTile box. To do that, look to the base of your model projects and snap on "master see". At that point select "new application" and select the sensors required for your application. At that point pick the sort of capacities and select how you require to yield your information. Spare the application and utilize the play catch to send your new application. Like that we have just manufactured our first test application.

When you are finished trying your thoughts, you can without much of a stretch beginning structure your real application with the STM32 Development Environment by utilizing the accessible capacity packs.

With this, I am finishing up my survey on the Sensor Tile advancement board. In general I figure this module will be extremely valuable to rapidly test and model your wearable gadget thoughts. Tell me your musings on this board in the remark segment and furthermore propose me a thought in the event that you might want me to attempt with this crate.

5. REMOTE DOORBELL UTILIZING ARDUINO ALONG WITH RF MODULE

We as a whole know about the wired doorbell frameworks which require wires and reasonable outlets for it to work agreeably. As the wired doorbell framework needs confounded wiring, it requires an accomplished individual to complete the work and it doesn't do great, in both working and appearance. Another issue with it is that, in case you require to introduce a wired doorbell framework for a current house, it needs more exertion and time for the establishment. Because of the temperature along with mugginess, and other natural components, wires are harmed and will prompt a short out. This is the place the remote doorbell framework gets into the image. In case the expense of the remote Doorbell framework is more, when contrasted with the wired door-bell framework, the standard support for the remote Doorbell framework is low when contrasted and the wired doorbell framework, which requires an accomplished individual for upkeep purposes. With regards to establishment, remote doorbell frameworks are easy to introduce and requires no experience individual for establishment. Moreover, remote doorbell frameworks have extra highlights like camera, video recorder, and so forth and look beautiful, and it very well may be effectively introduced in any piece of the house as it is totally remote.

In this task, we are going to assemble a Wireless Doorbell utilizing Arduino. We will have a catch which when squeezed will remotely play a song of our decision to demonstrate somebody is at the entryway. For remote network, we will utilize the 433 MHz RF module. When all is said in done, the RF module should consistently be joined by a decoder and encoder module, yet instead of the decoder and encoder module, we can likewise utilize a microcontroller, for example, Arduino which we are utilizing in this exercise. On the off chance that you need to assemble a basic wired Doorbell you can check this Doorbell utilizing 555 IC instructional exercises to construct one.

Equipment Required:

- RF module

- Arduino
- Bell

- Press button

- Breadboard

- Associating wires

433 MHz RF Module:

For our Arduino based Wireless Doorbell, we will utilize the 433 MHz Wireless RF modules. A RF module, which is a Radio Frequency module comprises of two modules, one which gets the information called recipient, and the one which transmits the information called transmitter.

Study the RF transmitter along with beneficiary by following the connection.

RF Transmitter:

A transmitter comprises of a SAW resonator, which is tuned to 433MHz recurrence, an exchanging circuit, and a couple of latent segments.

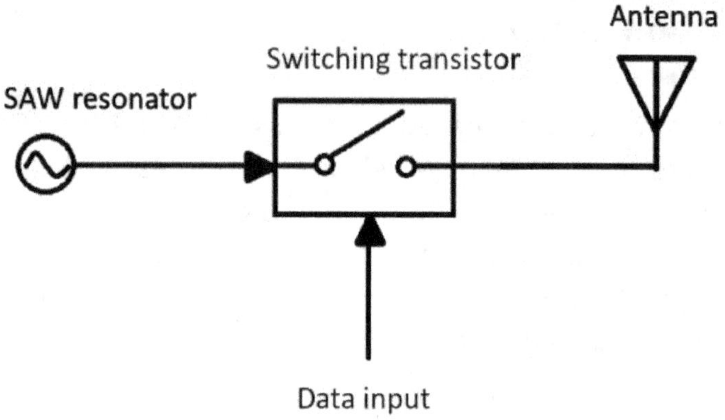

In the point when the contribution to the information pin is HIGH, the switch will go about as a short out and the oscillator runs which creates a fixed adequacy transporter wave and a fixed recurrence for some time of time't'. At the point when the contribution to the information pin is low, the switch goes about as an open-circuit and the yield will be zero. This is otherwise called Amplitude move keying (ASK). We will talk about additional on this later in this article

Collector Circuit:

A RF collector is a straightforward circuit that comprises of a RF tuned circuit, an enhancer circuit, and a stage lock circle circuit.

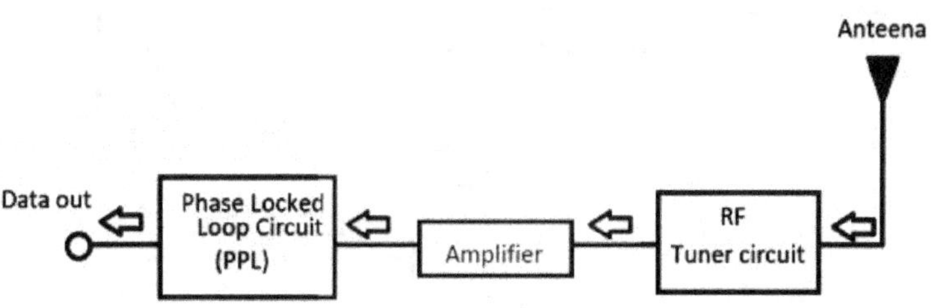

A RF tuner is utilized to tune the circuit to a specific recurrence, which needs to meet the transmitted recurrence. A speaker circuit is utilized to enhance a specific recurrence from every other sign and to build the affectability of the specific recurrence.

Stage Lock Loop Circuit:

A stage lock circle circuit (PLL) is a circuit that is utilized in sorts of gear in which we need an exceptionally steady recurrence from a low-recurrence reference signal. A PLL is a negative criticism framework that comprises of a voltage-controlled oscillator and a stage comparator associated so that the oscillator recurrence consistently coordinates the info signal as demonstrated as follows.

Phase loop lock circuit

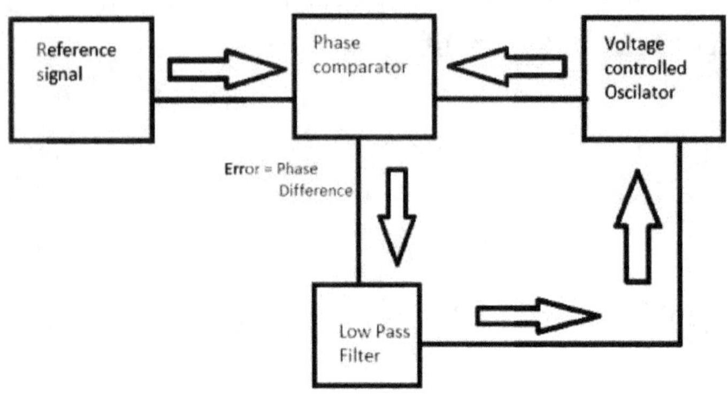

Feedback Circuit

In the PLL circuit two signs for example from the reference signal along with the sign from the voltage-controlled oscillator (VCO), is given as contributions to the stage identifier and the yield from the stage finder the distinction among both the information sources, and this yield is the stage contrast of both the signs. This yield contains recurrence parts, which are the aggregate and contrast of the signs. In this lines, this yield is given as contribution to the low pass channel, which permits just low frequencies, and doesn't permit the high-recurrence signs to go through. The yield of the low pass channel is taken care of to a voltage-controlled oscillator (VCO), and this information goes about as an incentive to the

VOC, which must be changed to diminish the stage distinction between both the signs. The adjustment in the VCO happens until the stage distinction is negligible, or the yield of the stage finder has a steady mistake yield. This outcomes on top of it lock circumstance.

With every one of these segments, the collector gets the sign from the recieving wire which is then tuned by RF tuned circuit and this feeble sign is enhanced utilizing OP-Amp, and this intensified sign is additionally utilized as contribution to PLL, which makes the decoder to bolt onto the approaching advanced bits which gives a yield which is less in commotion.

Balance:

Balance is a procedure of changing over information into electrical signs, and these regulated signs are utilized for transmission. We tweak the signs with the goal that we can isolate the vital sign from different signs. Without regulation, all the signs having similar frequencies will get blended, which will prompt mistake. There are many kinds of tweak the well known ones are Analog Modulation, Digital Modulation, Pulse Modulation, and Spread Spectrum.

Out of these the most famous one utilized in a remote transmission is computerized adjustment. The well known Digital adjustment methods are Amplitude

Shift Keying, Frequency Shift Keying, Phase Shift Keying, Orthogonal Amplitude Modulation.

Plentifulness Shift Keying (ASK) Modulation:

In Amplitude Shift key tweak, the sinusoidal transporter will continue producing ceaseless high-recurrence bearer, and the sign which is to be balanced will be in the double grouping, and these signs make the contribution to the changing circuit to be either high otherwise low.

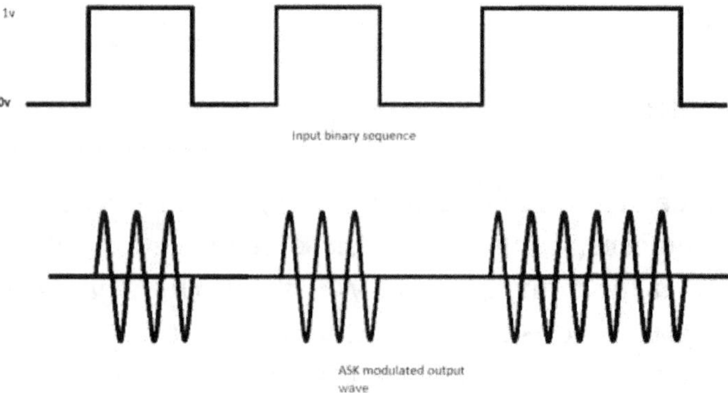

As appeared in the above figure, when the information is low, the switch will go about as an open circuit, along with the yield will be zero. In the point when the contribution to the switch is high, the yield will be the transporter signal.

Arduino RF Transmitter Schematic Diagram

Our remote doorbell undertaking will require a transmitter and collector circuit each with its own Arduino board. The Circuit outline for Doorbell Transmitter is demonstrated as follows

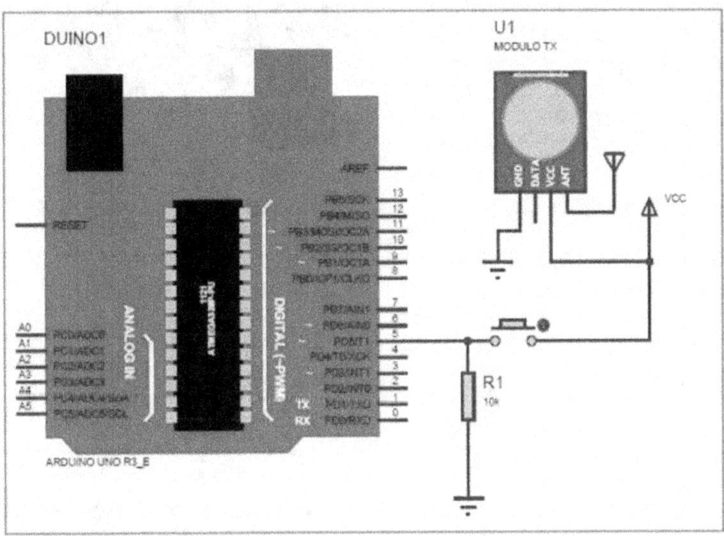

The Arduino pin 5 is combined with the one finish of the doorbell switch, and the opposite finish of the switch is combined with the gracefully voltage. A draw down resistor of 10kohm is combined with pin 5 as appeared in the fig. Pin 11 is combined with the information pin of the transmitter module. Vcc is combined with the flexibly voltage, and the ground pin of the transmitter module is grounded.

In here I utilized a breadboard for associating the modules, and a press button is used as a doorbell switch.

Arduino RF Receiver Schematic Diagram

Also, on the collector side, we have to utilize another Arduino board with the RF recipient module. At that point the Arduino Doorbell Receiver circuit additionally has a signal is to play some song when the catch is squeezed.

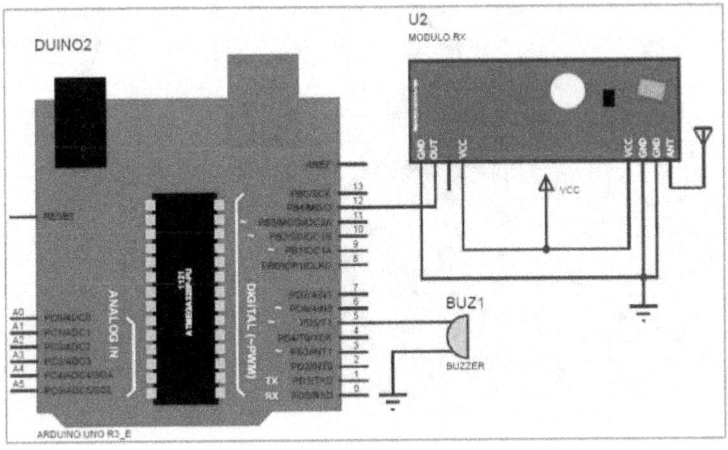

Here, we associate pin 7 of the Arduino to the bell positive terminal, along with the -ve terminal is grounded. A flexibly voltage of VCC is given to the recipient module, and the GND pin of the module is associated with the ground. The out pin of the collector module is combined with the twelfth pin of the Arduino.

The beneficiary module comprises of 4 pins in which one pin is grounded, and another pin is for giving VCC flexibly, and the staying two pins are utilized for information move. In the above chart, a bell is associated with the computerized seventh pin of the Arduino, and the twelfth pin of the Arduino is associated with the recipient module yield pin.

Arduino Transmitter Code Explanation

The total code for the Arduino transmitter part is given at the base of this page. The clarification of the code is as per the following.

These are the header records which are should have been incorporated to send or get the information utilizing the RF module. These libraries make the association among the Arduino and the module basic. Without these, you require to physically compose the code for interfacing the RF module with the Arduino. An item is made "driver" to get to the orders utilized for sending and getting the information. You can download the Radio Head Library for Arduino from Github.

```
#include <RH_ASK.h>

#include <SPI.h> // Not actually used but needed to compile

RH_ASK driver;
```

Serial.begin() is utilized to discover whether the RF transmitter module is working or not and I have introduced the PIN 5 (computerized pin 5) as an Input pin and this goes about as an entryway chime switch.

```
void setup()

{

    Serial.begin(9600); // Debugging only

    pinMode(5,INPUT);
```

This code is utilized to print the message "init fizzled" when the RF TX module doesn't instate at beginning of the program and this run just ones.

```
if (!driver.init())

    Serial.println("init failed");
```

The if work checks if the pin is rationale HIGH otherwise LOW, for example on the off chance that the doorbell switch is on the state or in an off state. The pointer msg contains the message which we require to send across a transmitter. One note is that we should know the quantity of characters we have to send. This will help recorded as a hard copy the collector code.

```
if(digitalRead(5)==HIGH){

const char *msg = "a";
```

The strlen() order checks the length of the message, which is 1 for this situation. The driver.send() orders sends the information to the tx module which are changed over into waves. The order driver.wait-PacketSent() is utilized to hold up until the information is sent.

```
driver.send((uint8_t *)msg, strlen(msg));

driver.waitPacketSent();
```

Arduino Receiver Code Explanation

The Receiver program is additionally given toward the finish of this page underneath the Transmitter code or it tends to be downloaded from here. You can straightforwardly utilize it with your equipment; the code clarification is as per the following.

These are the header records which are should have been incorporated to send or get the information utilizing the RF module. These libraries make the association among the Arduino and the RF module basic. Without these, you require to physically compose the code for associating the RF module with the Arduino.

```
#include <RH_ASK.h>

#include <SPI.h> // Not actually used but needed
to compile
```

These are the header documents that are made for the

code to liken the estimations of recurrence to a specific note and get the note esteems to get the melodic tone. In case you require to find about pitches.h or how to play the tune with Arduino and signal you can allude to this Melody utilizing Tone() Function instructional exercise.

```
#include "pitches.h" //add Equivalent frequency for musical note

#include "themes.h" //add Note vale and duration
```

An item is made "driver" to get to the orders utilized for sending and getting the information.

```
RH_ASK driver;
```

To print messages in the sequential screen. In this point the if condition checks if the introduction is fizzled or not.

```
void setup()

{
```

```
Serial.begin(9600);   // Debugging purpose

if (!driver.init())

    Serial.println("init failed");

  else

    Serial.println("done");
```

This entire code manages the notes, pitches, and term to be taken to the necessary song

```
void Play_Pirates()

{

 for (int thisNote = 0; thisNote < (sizeof(Pirates_note)/sizeof(int)); thisNote++) {

    int noteDuration = 1000 / Pirates_duration[thisNote];//convert duration to time delay

    tone(8, Pirates_note[thisNote], noteDuration);

    int pauseBetweenNotes = noteDuration * 1.05; // Here 1.05 is tempo, increase to play it slower

    delay(pauseBetweenNotes);
```

```
    noTone(8); //stop music on pin 8

    }

}
```

The order uint8_t buf[1] instates the buf as an unsigned number of length 8 bits, along with the size of the buf variable is 1, as I let you know before that we should what number of bits we sent along with getting the length of the buf variable in parallel structure.

```
void loop()

{

    uint8_t buf[1];

    uint8_t buflen = sizeof(buf);
```

This code checks whether we got the right information and if the got signal is right it plays the melody.

```
if (driver.recv(buf, &buflen)) // Non-blocking
```

```
Serial.println("Selected -> 'He is a Pirate'");

Play_Pirates();

Serial.println("stop");
```

Remote Arduino Doorbell Working

The transmitter module, alongside the Arduino is associated close to the entryway, and the beneficiary module, alongside Arduino, can be introduced in any piece of the room. In this point when somebody presses the switch, it sends the high heartbeat to the fifth pin of Arduino, which is associated close to the entryway alongside the transmitter module. In our Receiver code, we composed an order digitalRead(5), this order makes the Arduino, to continue perusing this pin. In this point when this pin gets HIGH, Arduino transmits information through the transmitter, and these signs are gotten by the beneficiary. The Arduino, which is combined with a ringer, peruses these signs, and when the ideal information is gotten, the if work is fulfilled, and the code will start the capacity, Play_Pirates() and the music will begin to play.

Expectation you comprehended the venture and delighted in getting the hang of something helpful.

Complete code is given underneath or it tends to be downloaded from this connection.

Code

Doorbell Transmitter Code

```
// ask_transmitter.pde
// -*- mode: C++ -*-
// Simple example of how to use RadioHead to trans-
mit messages
// with a simple ASK transmitter in a very simple way.
```

```
// Implements a simplex (one-way) transmitter with
an TX-C1 module
#include <RH_ASK.h>
#include <SPI.h> // Not actually used but needed to
compile
RH_ASK driver;
// RH_ASK driver(2000, 2, 4, 5); // ESP8266 or ESP32:
do not use pin 11
void setup()
{
  Serial.begin(9600);  // Debugging only
  pinMode(5,INPUT);
  if (!driver.init())
    Serial.println("init failed");
}
void loop()
{
  if(digitalRead(5)==HIGH){
  const char *msg = "a";
  driver.send((uint8_t *)msg, strlen(msg));
  driver.waitPacketSent();
  delay(200);
  }
}
```

Doorbell Receiver Code

```
#include <RII_ASK.h>
#include <SPI.h> // Not actualy used but needed to
compile
#include "pitches.h" //add Equivalent frequency for
musical note
```

```
#include "themes.h" //add Note vale and duration
RH_ASK driver;
void setup()
{
  Serial.begin(9600); // Debugging only
  if (!driver.init())
     Serial.println("init failed");
   else
    Serial.println("done");
}
void Play_Pirates()
{
    for (int thisNote = 0; thisNote < (sizeof(Pir-
ates_note)/sizeof(int)); thisNote++) {
    int noteDuration = 1000 / Pirates_duration[this-
Note];//convert duration to time delay
  tone(8, Pirates_note[thisNote], noteDuration);
   int pauseBetweenNotes = noteDuration * 1.05; //
Here 1.05 is tempo, increase to play it slower
  delay(pauseBetweenNotes);
  noTone(8); //stop music on pin 8
  }
}
void loop()
{
  uint8_t buf[1];
  uint8_t buflen = sizeof(buf);
  if (driver.recv(buf, &buflen)) // Non-blocking
  {
   Serial.println("Selected -> 'He is a Pirate' ");
   Play_Pirates();
```

```
  Serial.println("stop");
 }
}
```

◆ ◆ ◆

6. DRIVEN DISPLAY BOARD UTILIZING P10 LED MATRIX DISPLAY AND ARDUINO

Show publicizing assumes a very bringing in job in showcasing and there are a few promotion techniques like papers, banners, sparkle billboards, and so on yet computerized LED show sheets are getting famous these days as a result of their unwavering quality and focal points. In case they are somewhat costly still they are sturdy and adjustable, similar to the publicizing content can be modified effectively at whatever point required along with they can likewise be used as Digital Notice Board at any open spot. We recently utilized a 8x8 LED network with numerous sheets to control the content showed over it, today we will utilize the P10 show with Arduino.

Here we are gonna to use a 32x16 LED speck Matrix show module which is otherwise called P10 LED Display Module to show a looking over book by utilizing Arduino UNO. P10 modules can be fell to fabricate any size of the promoting board.

Equipment Needed

- Arduino UNO-1

- 16 Pin FRC connector-1

- 32*16 P10 LED show module-1

- Connectors

- 5V DC,3 AMP SMPS

Working of a P10 LED Matrix Module

A P10 LED Display Module is the most appropriate for planning any size of open air or indoor LED show promotion board. This board has a sum of 512 high brilliance LEDs mounted on a plastic lodging intended for best presentation results. Any number of such boards can be consolidated in any line and section structures to plan an alluring LED billboard.

The 32*16 module size implies that there are 32 LEDs in each line and 16 LEDs in every segment. So there is a sum of 512 quantities of LEDs present in every module unit.

Highlights of a P10 LED Matrix Module:

- **Splendor:** 3500-4500nits

- **Max Power Consumption:** 20W

- **Voltage Input:** DC 5V

- IP65 Waterproof

- 1W Pixel Configuration

- High Viewing Angle

- High Contrast Ratio

Pin depiction of P10 show module:

- **Empower:** This pin is used to manage the splendor of the LED board, by giving a PWM heartbeat to it.

- **A, B:** These are called multiplex select pins. They take computerized contribution to choose any multiplex lines.

- **Move clock (CLK), Store clock (SCLK) along with Data:** These are the typical move register control pins. Here a move register 74HC595 is utilized.

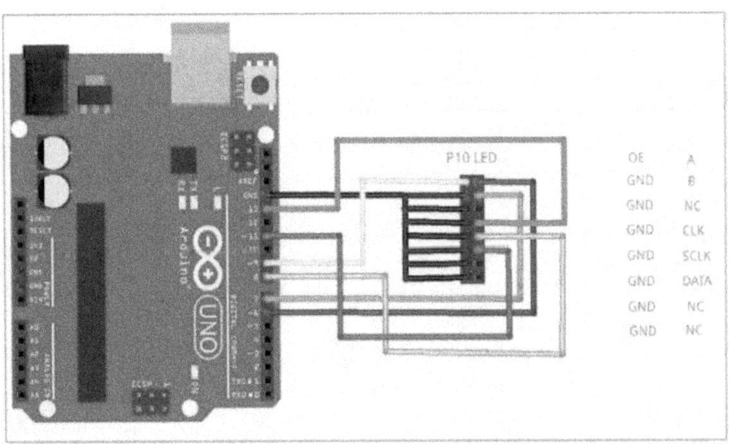

Circuit Diagram

Complete circuit chart for P10 module with Arduino is given underneath:

Arduino UNO and P10 show modules are interconnected according to the pin mapping are demonstrated as follows:

P10 LED Module	Arduino UNO
ENABLE	9
A	6
B	7
CLK	13
SCLK	8
DATA	11
GND	GND

Note: Connect the Power terminal of the P10 module to 5V DC SMPS independently. It is prescribed to interface a 5V, 3 Amp DC power gracefully to a solitary unit of P10 LED module. In the event that you are wanting to interface more quantities of the module, at that point increment your SMPS rating appropriately.

P10 LED Module programming with Arduino

After the fruitful finishing of the equipment arrangement, presently it's a great opportunity to program Arduino. Complete code for this 10 Led Display Arduino given toward the finish of this instructional exercise. The stepwise portrayal of the code is given underneath.

Above all else, remember all the reliant libraries for

the program. Here we are utilizing "DMD.h" Library for P10 drove activities, download this library from here and introduce it in Arduino IDE. After that incorporate the library for "TimerOne.h" which will be used for interfere with errands. This library can be installed from here.

At that point, incorporate all the necessary textual styles library, for our situation we are utilizing "Arial Black text style" for the presentation.

```
#include <SPI.h>

#include <DMD.h>

#include <TimerOne.h>

#include "SystemFont5x7.h"

#include "Arial_black_16.h"
```

In the following stage, characterize the quantity of lines and segments for the LED show board. For our condition we are utilizing just a single module, so ROW worth and COLUMN worth will be 1. At that point characterize the textual style name-Arial_Black_16 for the content looking in plain view board.

```
#define ROW 1

#define COLUMN 1

#define FONT Arial_Black_16

DMD led_module(ROW, COLUMN);
```

Capacity scan_module() which checks for any approaching information from Arduino side through the SPI Terminals. In case truly, in this point it will trigger an intrude on pin for doing certain occasions.

```
void scan_module()

{

  led_module.scanDisplayBySPI();

}
```

Inside arrangement(), instate the clock and append the hinder to the capacity scan_module. Capacity clearScreen(true) is utilized to set all pixels are off at first to clear the presentation board.

```
void setup()

{

  Timer1.initialize(2000);

  Timer1.attachInterrupt(scan_module);

  led_module.clearScreen( true );

}
```

In this point, to show a string in the module, select the text style utilizing selectFont() capacity and print a string message "Welcome" in the presentation utilizing drawMarquee() work.

```
  led_module.selectFont(FONT);

  led_module.drawMarquee("Welcome",25, (32 *
ROW), 0);
```

At last, to look over the content on the LED show load up move the whole message from Right to Left headings utilizing a specific timeframe.

```
long start = millis();

  long timming = start;

  boolean flag = false;

  while (!flag)

  {

   if ((timming + 20) < millis())

   {

     flag = led_module.stepMarquee(-1, 0);

     timming = millis();

   }

  }
```

So this is the way you can make a Scrolling Text Signboard utilizing Arduino and LED grid.

Complete code is given beneath.

Code

```
#include <SPI.h>
#include <DMD.h>
#include <TimerOne.h>
#include "SystemFont5x7.h"
#include "Arial_black_16.h"

#define ROW 1
#define COLUMN 1
#define FONT Arial_Black_16

DMD led_module(ROW, COLUMN);

void scan_module()
{
 led_module.scanDisplayBySPI();
```

```
}
void setup()
{
 Timer1.initialize(2000);
 Timer1.attachInterrupt(scan_module);
 led_module.clearScreen( true );
}
void loop()
{
  led_module.selectFont(FONT);
     led_module.drawMarquee("Welcome",25, (32 *
ROW), 0);
  long start = millis();
  long timming = start;
  boolean flag = false;
  while (!flag)
  {
   if((timming + 20) < millis())
   {
    flag = led_module.stepMarquee(-1, 0);
    timming = millis();
   }
  }
}
```

❖ ❖ ❖

7. PROGRAMMED BOTTLE FILLING SYSTEM UTILIZING ARDUINO

Programmed Bottle Filling Machines are most regularly utilized in refreshments and soda pop ventures. These machines utilize a transport line which is an affordable and quick approach to fill bottles. Generally PLCs are utilized for Automatic jug filling machines, however you can do an extremely essential and flexible container filler utilizing an Arduino. You can program the Arduino to consequently distinguish the container utilizing IR or ultrasonic sensor and permit the bottler to fill by halting the transport line for quite a while. Of course move the belt and stop when the following container is identified.

Here we are going to plan a model for Automatic Bottle Filling Machine utilizing Arduino Uno, transport line, solenoid valve, IR sensor, and Stepper engine. Belt transport is driven by a stepper engine at a consistent preset speed. The stepper engine will continue driving the belt until an IR sensor recognizes the nearness of a container on the belt. We utilized the IR sensor as an outside trigger. So at whatever point the IR sensor goes high it sends a trigger to Arduino to stop the engine and turn on the solenoid valve. A preset required postponement is as of now entered in the code for bottle filling. The Arduino will keep the solenoid valve on and stepper engine off until that predefined time. After that time, the solenoid valve kills the filling, and the transport begins moving so the following jug can be filled.

We recently utilized Arduino with Solenoid valve, IR Sensor and Stepper engine, so to study essential interfacing of Arduino with these segments, you can visit the connections.

Segments Required

- Arduino Uno
- Stepper Motor (Nema17)

- Transfer

- Solenoid Valve

- IR Sensor

- A4988 Motor Driver

- Battery

Circuit Diagram

The circuit chart for the Automatic Bottle Filling System utilizing Arduino is given beneath.

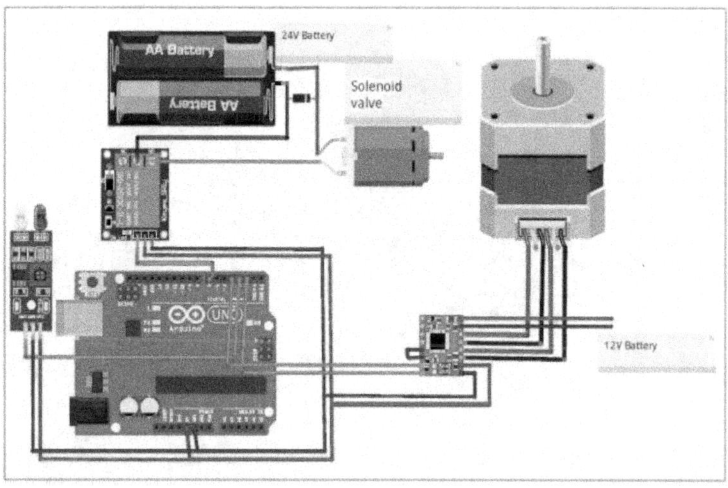

I have utilized Fritzing to draw the circuit graph. In this circuit, Solenoid Valve is associated with Arduino through the Relay module and the A4988 driver module is utilized to control the stepper engine. You can follow the How to Control Nema17 with Arduino and A4988 instructional exercise for more data on Nema17 and A4988 driver module.

The information pin of the Relay module is combined with pin 7 of Arduino. Bearing and Step pins of the A4988 module are associated with 2 and 4 pins of Arduino. In this undertaking, an IR sensor is utilized as an outer hinder to Arduino. In Arduino Uno, computerized pin 2 and 3 are the interfere with pins, so interface the Out pin of IR sensor to the third pin of Arduino. Solenoid Valve is fueled by a 24V force source, and Stepper engine is controlled by a 12V force source.

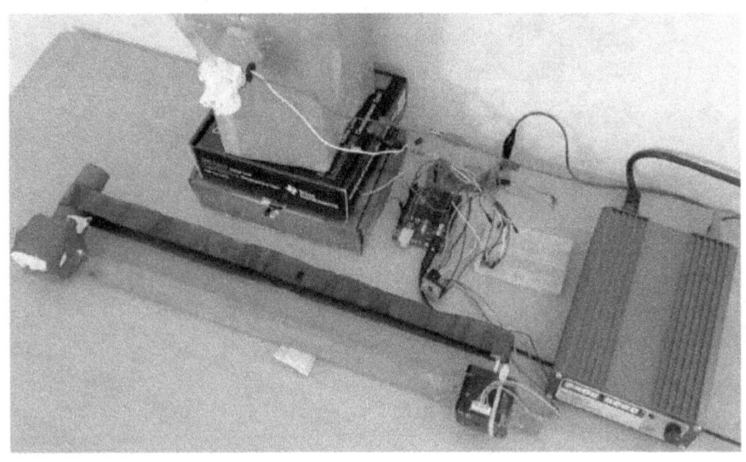

Arduino Program for Automatic Bottle Filling

The total program for this Automatic Bottle Filling System utilizing Arduino is given toward the end. Here I am clarifying some significant lines.

Start the program by including the stepper engine library. You can download the stepper engine library from here.

From that point onward, characterize the no of steps per upset for the stepper engine. For NEMA 17 stages for each unrest is 200.

```
#include <Stepper.h>

#define STEPS 200
```

Determine the pins to which Step and Direction pins of the engine driver module is associated. As the engine is associated through the driver module, characterize the engine interface type as Type1.

```
Stepper stepper(STEPS, 2, 4);

#define motorInterfaceType 1
```

Set the stepper engine speed.

```
stepper.setSpeed(500);
```

Characterize the Relay, step and course sticks as yield

```
pinMode(relay,OUTPUT);

pinMode(4,OUTPUT);

pinMode(2,OUTPUT);
```

The language structure for outside hinder in Arduino is given underneath:

```
attachInterrupt(digitalPinToInterrupt(pin),  ISR, mode);
```

Where:

digitalPinToInterrupt(pin): It is utilized to characterize the pin at which outer hinder is associated. In Arduino Uno Pin 2 and 3 are outside intrude on pins.

ISR: It is a capacity that is considered when an outer hinder is called.

Mode: Type of change to trigger on, e.g., falling, rising, and so on.

Get familiar with Arduino Interrupts by following the connection.

In attachInterrupt() work it is determined that pin

3 is the outside interfere with pin, and IR_detected work is called at whatever point IR sensor changes its state from is LOW to HIGH (RISING).

```
attachInterrupt(digitalPinToInterrupt(3),IR_detected,HIGH);
```

void IR_detected() is an ISR work that executes when the IR sensor goes high. So at whatever point the IR sensor goes high, this capacity runs the stepper engine for a couple of steps, and afterward stops the stepper engine and turns on the solenoid valve.

```
void IR_detected()     {

  stepper.step(150);

  digitalWrite(relay,HIGH);

  stepper.step(0);
```

Presently at last transfer the code to Arduino by associating it to the PC. The underneath picture shows our model for the Automatic Bottle Filling System utilizing Arduino.

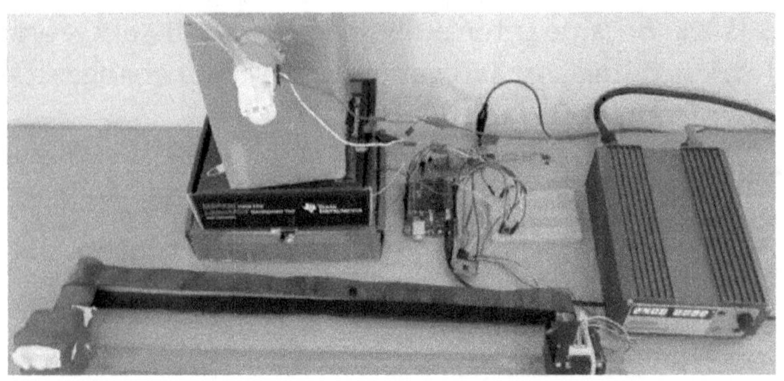

Complete code is given underneath.

Code

```
#include <Stepper.h>
#define STEPS 200
#define motorInterfaceType 1
Stepper stepper(STEPS, 2, 4);
int relay = 7;
int step_num = 700;
void setup() {
  Serial.begin(9600);
  pinMode(relay,OUTPUT);
  stepper.setSpeed(500);
  pinMode(4,OUTPUT);
```

```
 pinMode(2,OUTPUT);

    attachInterrupt(digitalPinToInterrupt(3),IR_detected,RISING);

}

boolean solenoid_on = false;

void loop() {

 if (solenoid_on)

 {

  delay(6000); //wait for 6 sec

  solenoid_on = false;

 }

 digitalWrite(relay,LOW);   // now relay is off condition (and motor is on condition)

 stepper.step(step_num);

 }

void IR_detected()      //ISR function excutes when IR sensor goes high.

 {

 Serial.println ("Interrupt Detected");

  stepper.step(150); //To run the stepper motor few steps before it stops

 digitalWrite(relay,HIGH); //to turn on solenoid
```

```
stepper.step(0); //to stop the stepper motor
solenoid_on = true;
}
```

❖ ❖ ❖

8. ARDUINO CURRENCY COUNTER UTILIZING IR AND COLOR SENSOR

In this venture we are going to chip away at an inventive arduino venture thought, where we can tally the paper money notes and figure their sum, by detecting the paper cash utilizing Color Sensor and Arduino. TCS230 shading sensor will be utilized for recognizing the money notes and, Arduino UNO for preparing the information and demonstrating the rest of the parity on 16x2 LCD.

Required Components:

- Arduino UNO

- TCS230 Color sensor

- IR sensor

- Breadboard

- 16*2 Alphanumeric LCD

- Associating Wires

TCS3200 Color Sensor Working

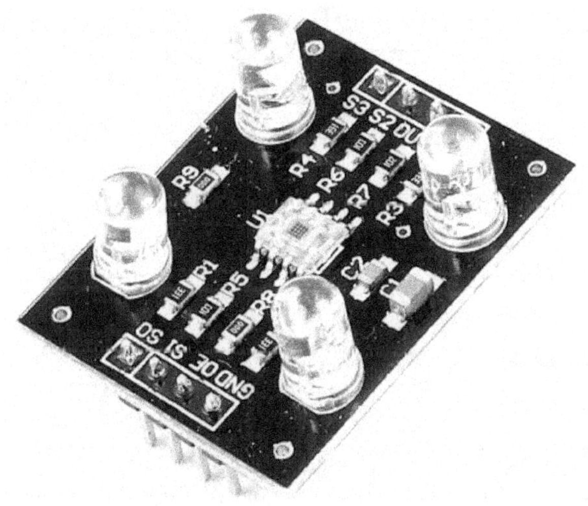

The TCS3200 shading sensor is utilized to detect a wide scope of hues. We beforehand interfaced TCS3200 shading sensor with Arduino and Raspberry pi, and furthermore manufactured some valuable undertakings like Color arranging machine.

TCS230 sensor has inbuilt infrared LEDs that are utilized to illuminate the article whose shading is to be recognized. This guarantees there will no effects of outer encompassing light on the item. This sensor peruses a photodiode of 8*8 exhibit, which contains 16 photodiodes with red channels, 16 with blue channels, 16 with green channels and 16 photodiodes with no channel. Every one of the sensor exhibits in these three clusters is chosen independently relying upon the prerequisite. Subsequently it is known as a programmable sensor. The module can be included to detect the specific shading and to leave the others. It contains channels for that choice reason. There is a fourth mode called 'no channel mode' where the sensor recognizes white light.

The yield sign of the TCS230 shading sensor is a square wave with a half obligation cycle and its recurrence is relative to the light force of the chose channel.

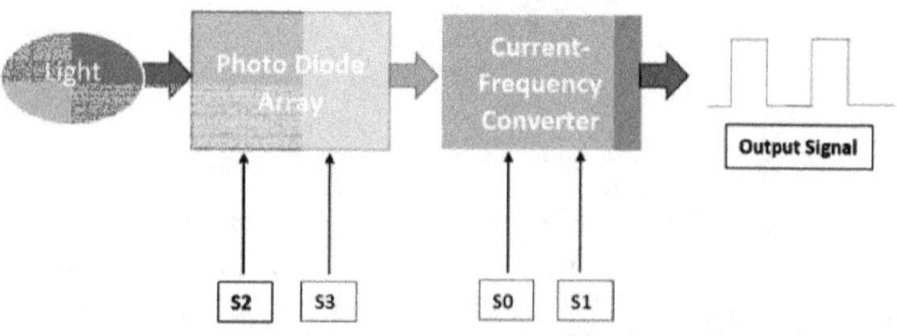

Pinout of TCS3200 Color Sensor:

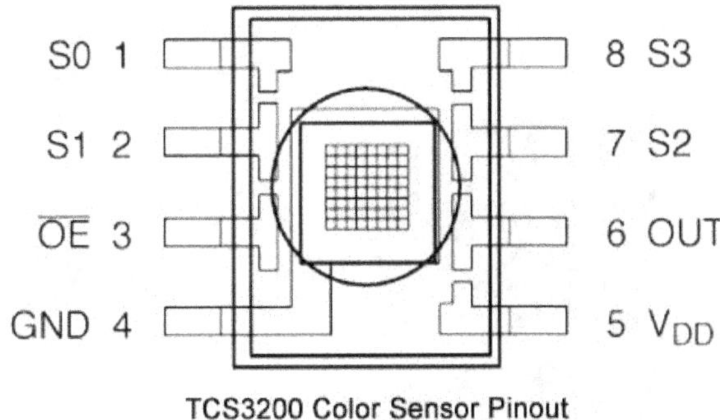

TCS3200 Color Sensor Pinout

VDD-Voltage flexibly pin of Sensor. It is provided with 5V DC.

GND-Ground reference pin of a shading sensor

S0, S1-Output recurrence scaling determination inputs

S2, S3-Photo-diode type determination inputs

OUT-Output pin of a shading sensor

OE-Enable pin for yield recurrence

We have additionally utilized an IR sensor in this venture, whose working can be comprehended by the accompanying connection.

Circuit Diagram

The following is the circuit outline for the Arduino Money Counter:

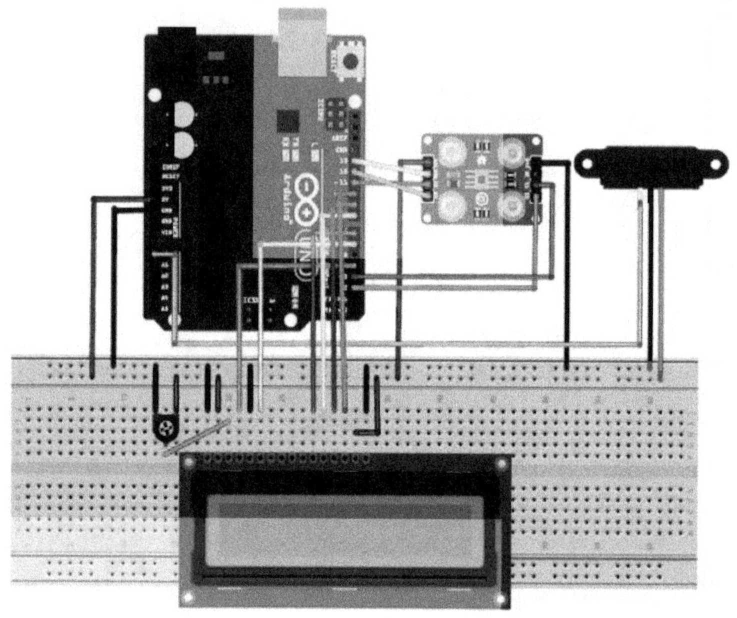

Here, I have made a little structure like a POS money swiping machine utilizing cardboards. In this structure, a shading sensor and an IR sensor are fixed with the cardboard like appeared in the picture underneath.

Here the IR sensor is used to detect the nearness of money inside the opening and in case there is a note, in this point the shading sensor will recognize the shade of the Note and send the shading an incentive to Arduino. Also, Arduino further figures the money esteem dependent on the shade of the note.

Code Explanation

Here the stepwise clarification of the total code is given underneath.

In the 1st place, remember all the libraries for the program. Here we just need the LCD library to be re-membered for the program. At that point proclaim all the factors utilized in the code.

```
#include <LiquidCrystal.h>

int OutPut = 13;
```

```
unsigned int frequency = 0;

LiquidCrystal lcd(4, 6, 7, 8, 9, 10);

int blue1;

int red1;

int green1;

int a = 0, b = 0;

int total = 1000;
```

Inside arrangement (), print the welcome message on LCD and characterize all the information bearings of advanced pins utilized in this venture. Next, set the yield recurrence scaling of the shading sensor, for my situation, it is set to 20% which can be set by giving HIGH heartbeat to S0 and LOW heartbeat to S1.

```
void setup()

{

  Serial.begin(9600);

  lcd.begin(16, 2);
```

```
  lcd.setCursor(0, 0);

  lcd.print(" Smart Wallet ");

  lcd.setCursor(0, 1);

  lcd.print("Hello World");

  delay(2000);

  lcd.clear();

  pinMode(2, OUTPUT);//S0

  pinMode(3, OUTPUT);//S1

  pinMode(11, OUTPUT);//S2

  pinMode(12, OUTPUT);//S3

  pinMode(13, INPUT);//OUT

  digitalWrite(2, HIGH);

  digitalWrite(3, LOW);
}
```

Inside unending circle (), read all the information

yields from the sensors. The yield from the IR sensor can be found by perusing the A0 pin and yield shading frequencies can be found by calling the individual capacities composed as red (), blue () and green (). At that point print every one of them on the Serial screen. This is required when we have to add another money to our task.

```
int sensor = digitalRead(A0);

int red1 = red();

int blue1 = blue();

int green1 = green();

Serial.println(red1);

Serial.println(blue1);

Serial.println(green1);

Serial.println("-----------------------------");
```

Next, compose all the conditions to check the yield recurrence of the shading sensor with the reference recurrence which we have set previously. In the event that it matches, at that point deducts the predefined sum from the wallet balance.

```
  if (red1>=20 && red1<=25 && blue1 >=30 &&
blue1 <=35 && green1 >=30 && green1 <=35 && a
== 0 && sensor == HIGH)

  {

   a = 1;

  }

 else if (sensor == LOW && a == 1)

  {

   a = 0;

   if(total>=10)

   {

   lcd.setCursor(0, 1);

   lcd.print("10 Rupees!!!");

   total=total-10;

   delay(1500);
```

```
    lcd.clear();

    }


  }
```

Here we have just set the conditions for 10 Rupees and 50 Rupees Note shading, you can set more conditions to identify all the more no. of money notes.

10 and 50 Rupees Note

Note: The recurrence yield might be diverse for your situation relying upon the outer lighting and sensor arrangement. So it is prescribed to check the yield recurrence of your money and set the reference esteem as needs be.

The underneath code will show the accessible parity in the wallet on the 16x2 LCD.

```
lcd.setCursor(0, 0);

lcd.print("Total Bal:");

lcd.setCursor(11, 0);

lcd.print(total);
```

```
delay(1000);
```

The accompanying capacity will get the yield shading recurrence of red substance in the cash. Thus, we can compose different capacities to get an incentive for blue and green shading substance.

```
int red()

{

  digitalWrite(11, LOW);

  digitalWrite(12, LOW);

  frequency = pulseIn(OutPut, LOW);

  return frequency;

}
```

So this is the manner by which an Arduino based Money counter can be constructed effectively utilizing barely any parts. We can additionally change it by coordinating some picture preparing and camera to recognize the cash utilizing the picture, that way it will be increasingly precise and will have the option to distinguish any money.

Code

```
int OutPut = 13;
unsigned int frequency = 0;
#include <LiquidCrystal.h>
LiquidCrystal lcd(4, 6, 7, 8, 9, 10);
int blue1;
int red1;
int green1;

int a = 0, b = 0;
int total = 1000;
void setup()
{
 Serial.begin(9600);
 lcd.begin(16, 2);
 lcd.setCursor(0, 0);
 lcd.print(" Smart Wallet ");
 lcd.setCursor(0, 1);
 lcd.print(" Hello world ");
 delay(2000);

 lcd.clear();

 pinMode(2, OUTPUT);//S0
 pinMode(3, OUTPUT);//S1
 pinMode(11, OUTPUT);//S2
 pinMode(12, OUTPUT);//S3
 pinMode(13, INPUT);//OUT

 digitalWrite(2, HIGH);
```

```
 digitalWrite(3, LOW);
}

void loop()
{
 int sensor = digitalRead(A0);
 int red1 = red();
 int blue1 = blue();
 int green1 = green();

 Serial.println(red1);
 Serial.println(blue1);
 Serial.println(green1);
 Serial.println("----------------------------");


  if(red1>=20 && red1<=25 && blue1 >=30 && blue1
<=35 && green1 >=30 && green1 <=35 && a == 0 &&
sensor == HIGH)
 {
  a = 1;
 }
 else if(sensor == LOW && a == 1)
 {
  a = 0;
  if(total>=10)
  {
  lcd.setCursor(0, 1);
  lcd.print("10 Rupees!!!");
  total=total-10;
  delay(1500);
  lcd.clear();
```

```
   }
 }
  if (red1 >= 25 && red1 <= 30 && blue1 >= 30 &&
blue1 <= 33 && green1 >= 25 && green1 <=30 && b ==
0 && sensor == HIGH)
  {
  b = 1;
  }
 else if(sensor == LOW && b == 1)
 {
  b = 0;
  if(total>=50)
  {
 lcd.setCursor(0, 1);
 lcd.print("50 Rupees!!!");
 total=total-50;
  delay(1500);
  lcd.clear();
  }
 }
 lcd.setCursor(0, 0);
 lcd.print("Total Bal:");
 lcd.setCursor(11, 0);
 lcd.print(total);
  delay(1000);
}

int red()
{
 digitalWrite(11, LOW);
 digitalWrite(12, LOW);
```

```
 frequency = pulseIn(OutPut, LOW);
 return frequency;
}
int blue()
{
 digitalWrite(11, HIGH);
 digitalWrite(12, HIGH);
 frequency = pulseIn(OutPut, LOW);
 return frequency;
}
int green()
{
 digitalWrite(11, LOW);
 digitalWrite(12, HIGH);
 frequency = pulseIn(OutPut, LOW);
 return frequency;
}
```

◆ ◆ ◆

9. NORDIC NRF52 DEVELOPMENT KIT – MEASURING TEMPERATURE ALONG WITH HUMIDITY UTILIZING BLUETOOTH LOW ENERGY

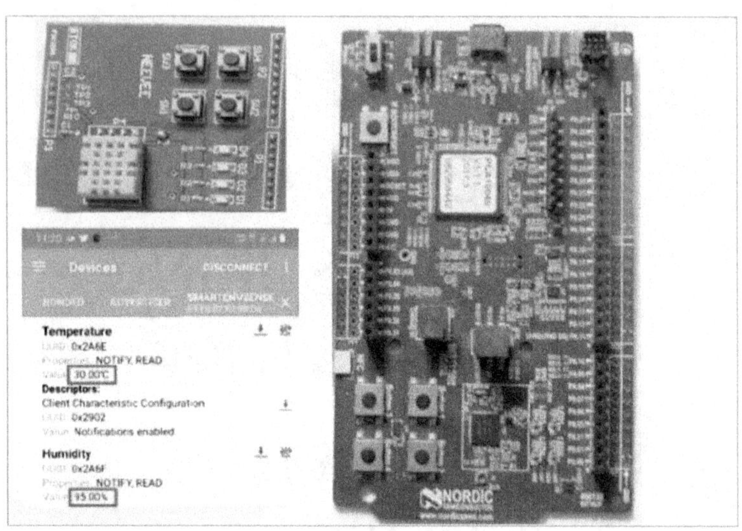

With Fitness Bands, Smartwatches along with other wearable gadgets getting progressively mainstream the usage of Bluetooth 5/Bluetooth Low Energy correspondence gauges is broadly being received. BLE causes us to trade information over a short separation with almost no force, which is extremely pivotal for battery-worked gadgets like wearables. It additionally encourages us to set up remote BLE work organizes, this component proves to be useful for home mechanization gadgets where different gadgets need to speak with one another in a shut situation. We have just utilized BLE with Raspberry

Pi and BLE with ESP32 to play out some fundamental BLE capacities. Specialists are exploring different avenues regarding BLE to structure versatile remote gadgets that can run for quite a while on little batteries and, there are various improvement packs accessible to work with BLE. In our ongoing audit on Arduino Nano 33, we likewise saw the board has nRF52840 with BLE capacities.

In this instructional exercise, we will investigate another energizing and mainstream advancement board called the nRF52 DK to gauge Temperature and Humidity utilizing BLE. As a matter of course, BLE Environment Sensing Profiles bolsters a wide scope of natural parameters yet this instructional exercise is constrained uniquely to temperature and mugginess esteems. This arrangement interfaces with a Smartphone over Bluetooth low vitality and gives a continuous update in regards to the ecological parameters i.e Temperature, Humidity. We will utilize the DHT1 sensor and the Temperature estimation will be finished with a goals of 0.01 degrees Celsius and Humidity estimation will be finished with a goals of 0.01 percent.

nRF52 Development Kit:

nRF52DK is a finished prototyping stage for Bluetooth Low Energy and 2.4 GHz Wireless Internet of Things application. The advancement unit bolsters different standard Nordic Toolchains like open-source, GCC and business coordinated improvement conditions like Keil, IAR and Segger Embedded Studio, and so forth. Nordic additionally gives an undeniable programming improvement pack for nRF52, that incorporates total help for nRF52DK.

nRF52DK is controlled with nRF52832 ARM Cortex-M4F Microcontroller, which is coordinated 512Kbytes of Flash Memor along with 64 Kbytes of SRAM. nRF52DK has a coordinated Segger J-Link On Board debugger, that gives a simpler and quicker troubleshooting without an outer/extra jtag investigate gadgets. It additionally incorporates the Arduino Uno Rev3 good connector, which underpins interfacing the simple and computerized contributions with the chip and it likewise incorporates standard correspondence conventions like, I2C (Inter-Integrated Circuit), SPI and UART. This advancement pack is planned with an incorporated in-assembled PCB radio wire that gives short-go remote correspondence utilizing Bluetooth Low Energy for interfacing with Smart Phone, Laptops and Tablets.

Segger Embedded Studio

To program the improvement board, we will utilize the Segger Embedded Studio with nRF52. Segger Embedded Studio is a ground-breaking C/C++ coordinated improvement condition (IDE) directed explicitly for installed frameworks advancement. This gives a total across the board arrangement containing everything required for implanted C programming, improvement and investigating. This incorporates total work process for implanted frameworks programming and improvement, highlighted with venture the executives, editorial manager, debugger supporting ARM Cortex gadgets. This ground-breaking and simple to utilize IDE is totally free for Nordic clients with full permit with no code size limitations. The IDE can be installed from the connection given beneath,

Install Segger Embedded Studio

DHT11 with nRF52DK

DHT11 is a full-included Temperature along with Humidity Sensor with a Resistive Type Humidity

Measurement Component along with a NTC type Temperature Measurement Component. It offers phenomenal quality, quicker reaction, along with cost-adequacy. As a matter of course, all DHT11 sensors are adjusted in the lab which prompts outrageous exactness and unwavering quality. It conveys utilizing Single-Wire Serial Interface framework and different determinations are given beneath

Particulars of DHT11:

- Stickiness Range: 20 – 90 % RH

- Temperature Range: 0 – 50°c

- Stickiness Accuracy: ±5%RH

- Temperature Accuracy: ±2?

Timing Diagram of DHT11:

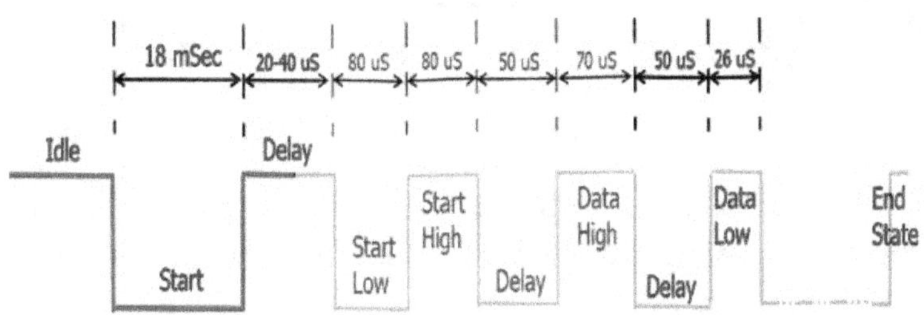

Perusing the information from the DHT11 sensor is generally straightforward utilizing the planning outline appeared previously. The system is like any controller and we have just utilized this sensor with other advancement stages like

- DHT11 Sensor with Raspberry Pi

- DHT11 Sensor with PIC16F877A

- DHT11 Sensor with STM32F103C8

- DHT11 sensor with NodeMCU

To interface the DHT11 Temperature along with Humidity sensor with nRF52 Development Kit, follow the association graph given beneath.

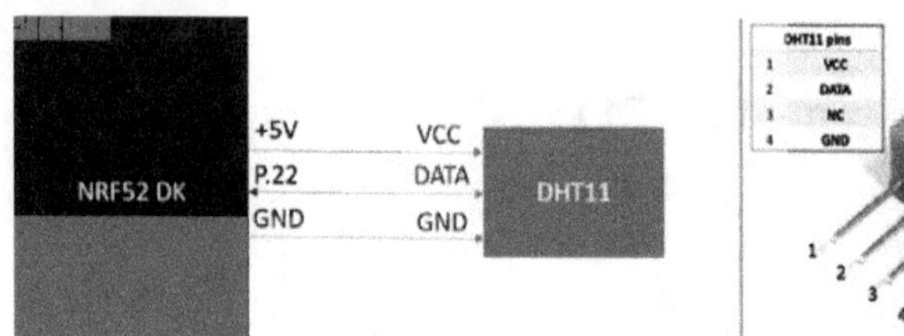

I am utilizing a connector module to associate the sensor to my board, so my last set-up resembles this

Stream Chart for speaking with DHT11:

The beneath stream graph clarifies the program legitimate stream that we will use to impart somewhere in the range of nRF52DK and DHT11

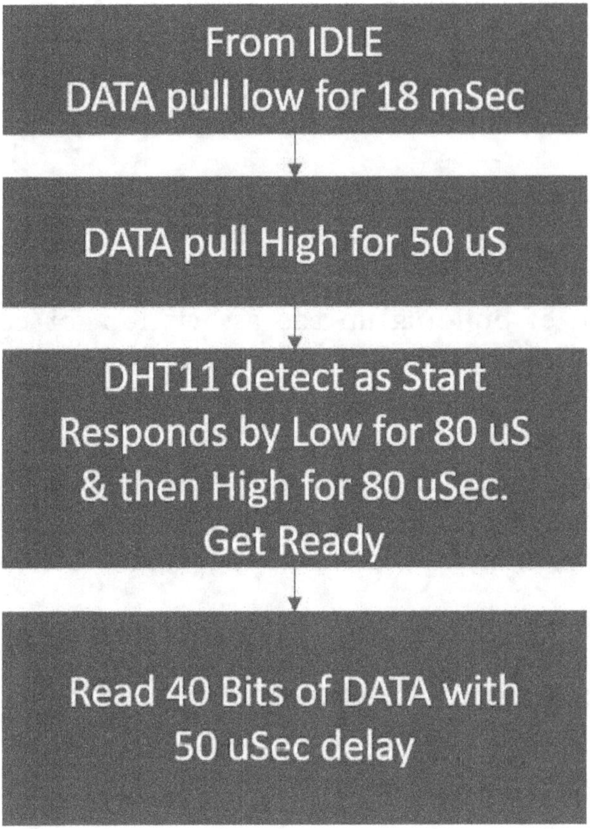

From IDLE
DATA pull low for 18 mSec
DATA pull High for 50 uS
DHT11 detect as Start
Responds by Low for 80 uS
& then High for 80 uSec.
Get Ready
Read 40 Bits of DATA with
50 uSec delay

Information Format:

Byte 1
RH Integer
Byte 2
RH Decimal
Byte 3
T Integer
Byte 4
T Decimal
Byte 5
Check Sum

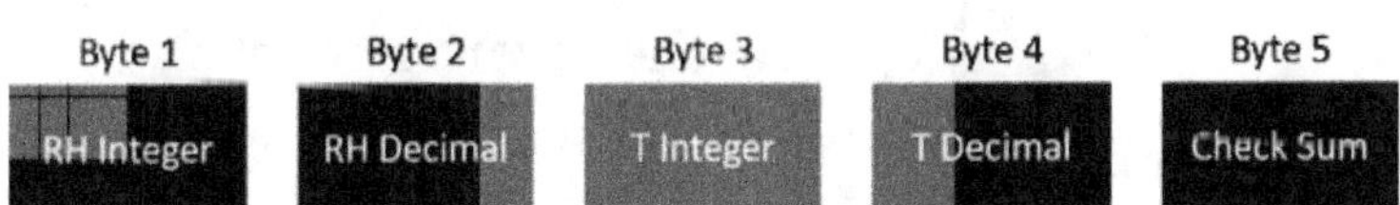

How to function with Bluetooth Low Energy (BLE)?

So as to see how to utilize BLE include, we need

to comprehend a couple of essential phrasings that are clarified underneath, you can likewise peruse the ESP32 BLE article to find out about BLE

Conventional Access Profile (GAP)

Conventional Access Profile holds the total obligation of building up the association for correspondence between BLE fringe and Central Devices. Hole additionally gives different methods including gadget filtering/revelation, interface layer association foundation, connect end, handshaking of security highlights and undeniable gadget arrangement. Hole works in the accompanying gadget states

GAP States	Description
Standby	Device initial state upon reset
Advertiser	Device advertising with data that helps for initiator scanning
Scanner	Receives the advertisement and sends scan request to the advertiser
Initiator	Sends a connection request to establish a link

Slave / Master	On connection, device as a slave if advertiser, master if an initiator

Conventional Attribute Profile Layer (GATT)

GATT stands short for Generic Attribute Profile Layer, it is answerable for information correspondence between two BLE gadgets (Peripheral along with Central). Information correspondence is described as qualities, which impart and store the information. BLE gadget assumes two unique jobs for gadget correspondence given beneath,

- GATT Server contains the qualities data which will be utilized to peruse and compose. In our instructional exercise, the DHT11 sensor, and the dev. the pack is our GATT Server.

- GATT Client peruses and composes the information from/to the GATT Server. The cell phone is a GATT Client that peruses and composes the information into our sensor board.

Bluetooth SIG

Bluetooth Special Interest Group (SIG) is the principles association that screens the improvement of Bluetooth measures and the authorizing the Bluetooth advancements. The SIG bunch doesn't create or sell any Bluetooth items. It characterizes the Bluetooth determination and normalization. They characterize the Unique Identifier for Bluetooth low vitality profile and separate attributes. The GATT Profile particulars can be found at the connection underneath

GATT Profile details

In light of GATT Specification given in the above connection, we have gathered the one of a kind identifiers required for our undertaking which is classified underneath.

Profile / Characteristics	UUID
GAP (Generic Access)	0x1800
GATT (Generic Attribute)	0x1801
ESS (Environment Sensing)	0x181A
Temperature	0x2A6E
Humidity	0x2A6F

BLE Service/Characteristics Diagram

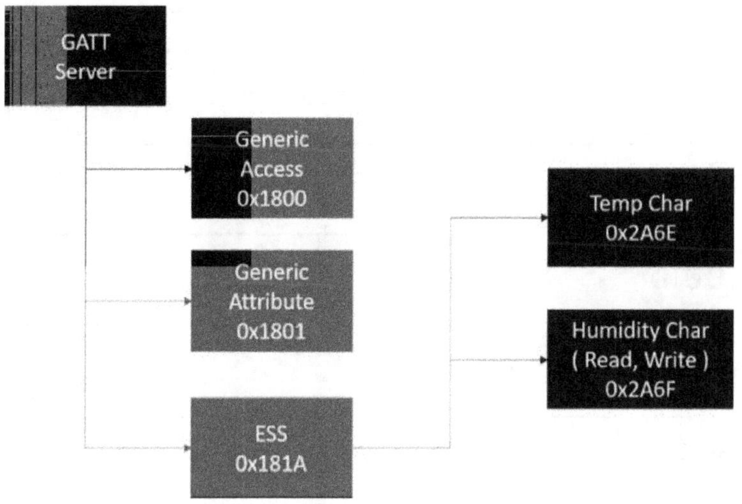

BLE UUIDs

UUID	16 bit value	128 bit UUID
ESS Service	0x181A	0000181A-0000-0000-0000-00000000000
Temp Char	0x2A6E	00002A6E-0000-0000-0000-00000000000
Humidity Char	0x2A6F	00002A6F-0000-0000-0000-00000000000

Temperature Characteristics

Property	Description

Unit	Degree Celsius with a resolution of 0.01 degree
Format	sint16
UUID	0x2A6E
Decimal Exponent	2
Read	Mandatory

Mugginess Characteristics

Property	Description
Unit	Percentage with a resolution of 0.01 percent
Format	uint16
UUID	0x2A6F
Decimal Exponent	2
Read	Mandatory

nRF52 BLE Program Explanation

We will utilize the nRF5 SDK so as to program our nRF52 Development unit. nRF5 SDK is a finished programming advancement unit coordinated with various Bluetooth Low Energy profiles, GATT Serializer and driver support for all the peripherals on nRF5 arrangement SoCs. This SDK causes engineers to fabricate full-included, dependable and secure Bluetooth low vitality applications with nRF52 and nRF51 arrangement of microcontrollers. The total program can be downloaded from here, the code clarification is as per the following.

Design the DHT11 DATA pin as contribution at nrf52 with pull up empower. Pin status ought to be high to affirm that nRF52 gives legitimate PULLUP to the DHT11 information pin

```
/* set to input and check if the signal gets pulled up */

  Data_SetInput();

  DelayUSec(50);

  if(Data_GetVal()==0){

    return DHT11_NO_PULLUP;
```

```
}
```

Produce START signal from nRF52 Microcontroller and check for recognize signal.

```
/* send start signal */

  Data_SetOutput();

  Data_ClrVal();

  DelayMSec(20); /* keep signal low for at least 18
ms */

  Data_SetInput();

  DelayUSec(50);

  /* check for acknowledge signal */

  if (Data_GetVal()!=0) { /* signal must be pulled low
by the sensor */

    return DHT11_NO_ACK_0;

  }

  /* wait max 100 us for the ack signal from the sen-
```

```c
sor */

 cntr = 18;

 while(Data_GetVal()==0) { /* wait until signal goes
up */

        DelayUSec(5);

  if(--cntr==0) {

    return DHT11_NO_ACK_1; /* signal should be
up for the ACK here */

  }

}

 /* wait until it goes down again, end of ack se-
quence */

 cntr = 18;

 while(Data_GetVal()!=0) { /* wait until signal goes
down */

        DelayUSec(5);

  if(--cntr==0) {
```

```c
    return DHT11_NO_ACK_0; /* signal should be
down to zero again here */

    }

}
```

Presently read the 40 bits of information that contains 2 bytes of temperature, 2 bytes of dampness and 1 byte of a checksum.

```c
/* now read the 40 bit data */

  i = 0;

  data = 0;

  loopBits = 40;

  do {

    cntr = 11; /* wait max 55 us */

    while(Data_GetVal()==0) {

      DelayUSec(5);

      if(--cntr==0) {
```

```c
      return DHT11_NO_DATA_0;

    }

  }

  cntr = 15; /* wait max 75 us */

  while(Data_GetVal()!=0) {

    DelayUSec(5);

    if(--cntr==0) {

      return DHT11_NO_DATA_1;

    }

  }

  data <<= 1; /* next data bit */

  if(cntr<10) { /* data signal high > 30 us ==> data bit 1 */

    data |= 1;

  }

  if((loopBits&0x7)==1) { /* next byte */
```

```
    buffer[i] = data;

   i++;

   data = 0;

  }

 } while(--loopBits!=0);
```

Approve the information with the assistance of Checksum.

```
/* test CRC */

 if         ((uint8_t)(buffer[0]+buffer[1]+buffer[2]+
buffer[3])!=buffer[4]) {

   return DHT11_BAD_CRC;

 }
```

Control and store the temperature and mugginess

```
 /* store data values for caller */

 humidity = ((int)buffer[0])*100+buffer[1];
```

```
temperature = ((int)buffer[2])*100+buffer[3];
```

Introduce the nRF5 SDK Logger administration. nRF52 SDK is highlighted with a logging control interface called nrf_log and utilizes the default backend for logging the data. The default backend will be a sequential port. Here we introduce both nrf_log control interface along with nrf_log default backends also.

```
ret_code_t err_code = NRF_LOG_INIT(NULL);

APP_ERROR_CHECK(err_code);

NRF_LOG_DEFAULT_BACKENDS_INIT();
```

nRF52 SDK has application clock usefulness. The application clock module empowers to make different clock examples dependent on RTC1 fringe. Here we instate the nRF5 application clock module. In this arrangement, two application clocks are utilized for commercial and information update interim.

```
ret_code_t err_code = app_timer_init();

APP_ERROR_CHECK(err_code);
```

nRF52 SDK has the full component power the executives module since BLE gadgets need to work for numerous months on a Coin cell battery. Force the executives assumes an imperative job in BLE applications. nRF52 power the board module totally handles the equivalent. Here we instate Power Management module of nRF5 SDK

```
ret_code_t err_code;

err_code = nrf_pwr_mgmt_init();

APP_ERROR_CHECK(err_code);
```

nRF52 SDK has an in-constructed Nordic Soft Device firmware hex record, which highlights Bluetooth low vitality focal and fringe stack. This profoundly qualified convention stack incorporates GATT, GAP, ATT, SM, L2CAP, and Link Layer. Here we follow the in-statement grouping, that introduced nRF5 BLE Radio Stack (Nordic Soft Device)

```
ret_code_t err_code;

err_code = nrf_sdh_enable_request();
```

```
APP_ERROR_CHECK(err_code);

// Configure the BLE stack using the default settings.

// Fetch the start address of the application RAM.

uint32_t ram_start = 0;

err_code = nrf_sdh_ble_default_cfg_set(APP_BLE_
CONN_CFG_TAG, &ram_start);

APP_ERROR_CHECK(err_code);

// Enable BLE stack.

err_code = nrf_sdh_ble_enable(&ram_start);

APP_ERROR_CHECK(err_code);

// Register a handler for BLE events.

NRF_SDH_BLE_OBSERVER(m_ble_observer,
APP_BLE_OBSERVER_PRIO,          ble_evt_handler,
NULL);
```

Hole is answerable for gadget filtering/revelation, connect foundation, interface end, inception of security highlights and setup. Hole has highlighted with key association parameters like association interim, slave inertness, management break, and so forth. Herewith introducing the Generic Access Profile association parameters

```
ret_code_terr_code;

ble_gap_conn_params_tgap_conn_params;

ble_gap_conn_sec_mode_t sec_mode;

BLE_GAP_CONN_SEC_MODE_SET_OPEN(&sec_mode);

err_code = sd_ble_gap_device_name_set(&sec_mode,

(const uint8_t *)DEVICE_NAME,

strlen(DEVICE_NAME));

APP_ERROR_CHECK(err_code);

memset(&gap_conn_params, 0, sizeof(gap_conn_params));

gap_conn_params.min_conn_interval = MIN_CONN_INTERVAL;

gap_conn_params.max_conn_interval = MAX_CONN_INTERVAL;
```

```
gap_conn_params.slave_latency= SLAVE_LATENCY;

gap_conn_params.conn_sup_timeout=        CONN_
SUP_TIMEOUT;

err_code      =      sd_ble_gap_ppcp_set(&gap_conn_
params);

APP_ERROR_CHECK(err_code);
```

GATT is answerable for information correspondence between BLE fringe and focal gadgets. nRF52 GATT module is useful for arranging and monitoring the most extreme ATT_MTU size. Here we introduce the nRF52 SDK Generic Attribute Module,

```
ret_code_t err_code = nrf_ble_gatt_init(&m_gatt,
NULL);

APP_ERROR_CHECK(err_code);
```

GATT does information correspondence as administrations and attributes. Here we introduce the GATT condition detecting administrations, which incorporates the introduction of attributes like temperature and mugginess.

```
ret_code_terr_code;

nrf_ble_qwr_init_t qwr_init = {O};

// Initialize Queued Write Module.

qwr_init.error_handler = nrf_qwr_error_handler;

err_code = nrf_ble_qwr_init(&m_qwr, &qwr_init);

APP_ERROR_CHECK(err_code);

m_ess.notif_write_handler    =    ble_ess_notif_write_handler;

err_code = ble_ess_init(&m_ess);

APP_ERROR_CHECK(err_code);
```

Promoting assumes a fundamental job in the BLE application condition. Notice parcels incorporate the data of address type, publicizing type, promoting information, gadget producer explicit information, and output reaction information. nRF52 SDK included with a publicizing module. Here we do instatement of the promoting module with the parameters.

```
ret_code_terr_code;

ble_advdata_t advdata;

ble_advdata_t srdata;

ble_uuid_t  adv_uuids[]  =  {{ESS_UUID_SERVICE,
BLE_UUID_TYPE_BLE}};

// Build and set advertising data.

memset(&advdata, 0, sizeof(advdata));

advdata.name_type= BLE_ADVDATA_FULL_NAME;

advdata.include_appearance = true;

advdata.flags=   BLE_GAP_ADV_FLAGS_LE_ONLY_
GENERAL_DISC_MODE;

memset(&srdata, 0, sizeof(srdata));

srdata.uuids_complete.uuid_cnt    =    sizeof(ad-
v_uuids) / sizeof(adv_uuids[0]);

srdata.uuids_complete.p_uuids= adv_uuids;

err_code  =  ble_advdata_encode(&advdata,  m_
```

```
adv_data.adv_data.p_data,    &m_adv_data.adv_
data.len);

APP_ERROR_CHECK(err_code);

err_code = ble_advdata_encode(&srdata, m_adv_
data.scan_rsp_data.p_data, &m_adv_data.scan_r-
sp_data.len);

APP_ERROR_CHECK(err_code);

ble_gap_adv_params_t adv_params;

// Set advertising parameters.

memset(&adv_params, 0, sizeof(adv_params));

adv_params.primary_phy= BLE_GAP_PHY_1MBPS;

adv_params.duration= APP_ADV_DURATION;

adv_params.properties.type    =    BLE_GAP_ADV_
TYPE_CONNECTABLE_SCANNABLE_UNDIRECTED;

adv_params.p_peer_addr= NULL;

adv_params.filter_policy= BLE_GAP_ADV_FP_ANY;

adv_params.interval= APP_ADV_INTERVAL;
```

```
err_code = sd_ble_gap_adv_set_configure(&m_ad-
v_handle, &m_adv_data, &adv_params);

APP_ERROR_CHECK(err_code);
```

BLE Connection will be taken care of and observed with different association parameters like first association params update delay, next successive postponements, update tally, association occasion handler callback capacity and association mistake callback occasion handler. Here we do introduction BLE Connection foundation parameters and a callback occasion handler for association occasions and mistake occasions.

```
ret_code_terr_code;

ble_conn_params_init_t cp_init;

memset(&cp_init, 0, sizeof(cp_init));

cp_init.p_conn_params= NULL;

cp_init.first_conn_params_update_delay = FIRST_
CONN_PARAMS_UPDATE_DELAY;

cp_init.next_conn_params_update_delay= NEXT_
CONN_PARAMS_UPDATE_DELAY;
```

```
cp_init.max_conn_params_update_count=    MAX_
CONN_PARAMS_UPDATE_COUNT;

t_on_notify_cccd_handle=    BLE_GATT_HANDLE_
INVALID;

cp_init.disconnect_on_fail= false;

cp_init.evt_handler= on_conn_params_evt;

cp_init.error_handler=    conn_params_error_hand-
ler;

err_code = ble_conn_params_init(&cp_init);

APP_ERROR_CHECK(err_code);
```

After the finish of the instatement of the framework, here we start with publicizing the BLE gadget name and ability data. From here, this fringe can be view over the cell phone Ble filter list.

```
ret_code_terr_code;

err_code  =  sd_ble_gap_adv_start(m_adv_handle,
APP_BLE_CONN_CFG_TAG);

APP_ERROR_CHECK(err_code);
```

The principle circle runs over the interim of 2 seconds, read the temperature and moistness and updates to an associated savvy gadget utilizing either read or notice

```
for (;;)

{

uint16_t temperature, humidity;

DHTxx_ErrorCode dhtErrCode;

idle_state_handle();

if(updtmrexp) {

dhtErrCode = DHTxx_Read(&temperature, &humidity);

if(dhtErrCode == DHT11_OK) {

NRF_LOG_INFO("Temperature: %d  Humidity: %d
\n", temperature, humidity);

if(temp_notif_enabled) {

ble_ess_notify_temp(m_conn_handle, &m_ess, tem-
```

```
 perature);

}else{

ble_ess_update_temp(&m_ess, temperature);

}

if(humid_notif_enabled){

ble_ess_notify_humid(m_conn_handle,     &m_ess,
humidity);

}else{

ble_ess_update_humid(&m_ess, humidity);

}

}

updtmrexp=false;

}

}
```

Testing our Program utilizing nRF Connect

nRF Connect is an amazing Bluetooth low vitality device that permits to examine and investigate the BLE empowered peripherals. nRF Connect for portable backings a wide scope of Bluetooth SIG embraced standard profiles. We can confirm our program by utilizing this, in the wake of introducing the application we can combine the nRF52 board with our telephone by examining for BLE gadgets on the application. Inside the Environmental detecting characteristic, we can see the temperature and mugginess esteems getting refreshed as appeared in the beneath pictures.

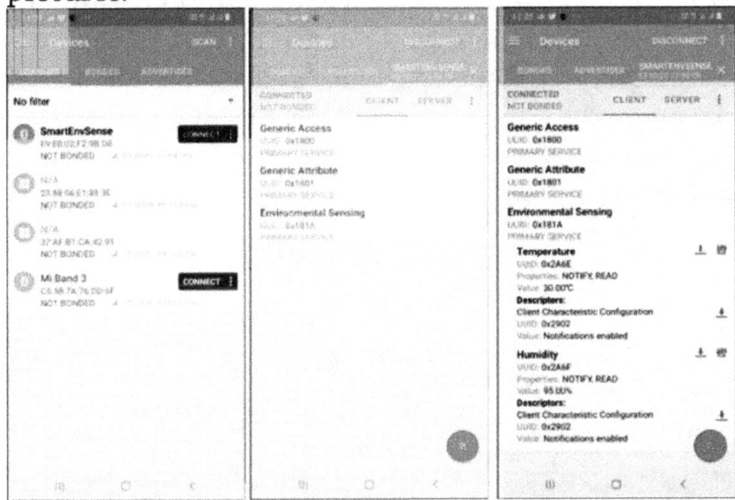

Smart BLE Device Scanning	Smart Environ Sensor Connection	Temp & Humidity Sensing

Complete code for this venture can be downloaded from here. I trust you delighted in the manufacture and got the hang of something valuable. Tell me in the remark area about your involvement in the nRF52 Development unit. In case you have few other specialized inquiries please utilize our discussions.

Creator Information

Hariharan Veerappan is a free advisor having over 15 years of involvement with inserted item advancement. He gives counseling administrations in inserted firmware/Linux improvement, he likewise gives corporate and web based preparing. Hariharan holds a Bachelor of Engineering certificate in the order of Electronics along with Communication Engineering, through his articles and instructional exercises he imparts his experience and considerations to the perusers.

10. HAND GESTURE CONTROLLED ROBOTIC ARM UTILIZING ARDUINO NANO

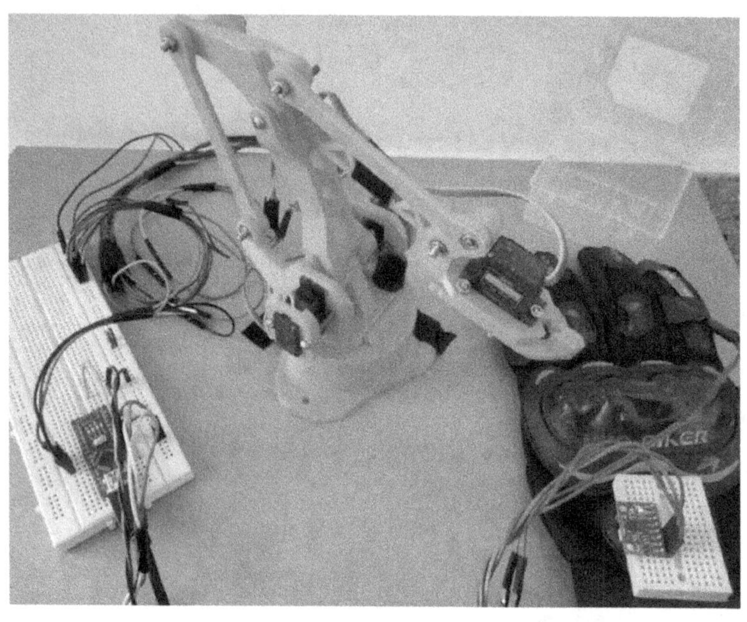

Automated Arms are one of the interesting design-ing manifestations and it is continually intriguing to watch these things tilt and container to complete complex things simply like a human arm would. These automated arms can be normally found in businesses at the sequential construction system per-forming extraordinary mechanical work like welding, boring, painting, and so on., as of late progressed automated arms with high accuracy are likewise being created to perform complex careful activities. Beforehand we 3D printed a mechanical Arm and manufactured a DIY Pick along with Place Robotic arm utilizing ARM7 Microcontroller. We will again utilize a similar 3D printed Robotic Arm to make a Hand motion controlled mechanical ARM utilizing Arduino Nano, MPU6050 Gyroscope and flex sensor.

This 3D printed mechanical arm position is controlled through a hand glove that is appended with a MPU6050 Gyroscope and a flex sensor. The Flex sensor is used to control the gripper servo of Robotic Arm and the MPU6050 is utilized for the development of automated in X and Y-pivot. On the off chance that you don't have a printer, you can likewise assemble your arm with basic cardboard as we worked for our Arduino Robotic Arm Project. For motivation, you can likewise allude to the Record and Play Robotic Arm that we manufactured before utilizing Arduino.

Prior to broadly expounding, first, we should find out about the MPU6050 sensor and flex sensor.

MPU6050 Gyroscopic and Accelerometer Sensor?

MPU6050 depends on Micro-Mechanical Systems (MEMS) innovation. This sensor has a 3-pivot accelerometer, a 3-hub spinner, and an in-manufactured temperature sensor. It very well may be used to quantify parameters like Acceleration, Velocity, Orientation, Displacement, along with etc. We have beforehand interfaced MPU6050 with Arduino along with Raspberry pi along with furthermore manufactured a couple of tasks utilizing it like-Self Balancing robot, Arduino Digital Protractor, along with Arduino Inclinometer.

Highlights in MPU6050 Sensor:

- Correspondence: I2C convention with configurable I2C Address

- Information Power Supply: 3-5V

- Worked in 16-piece ADC gives high precision

- Worked in DMP gives high computational force

- Can be used to interface with other I2C gadgets like a magnetometer

- In-constructed temperature sensor

Pin-Out subtleties of MPU6050:

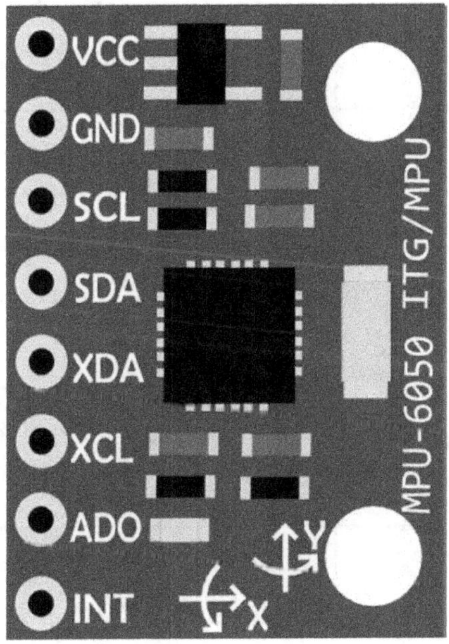

Pin	Usage
Vcc	Provides power for the module, can be +3V to +5V. Typically +5V is used
Ground	Connected to Ground of system
Serial Clock (SCL)	Used for providing clock pulse for I2C Communication
Serial Data (SDA)	Used for transferring Data through I2C communication
Auxiliary Serial Data (XDA)	Can be used to interface other I2C modules with MPU6050
Auxiliary Serial Clock (XCL)	Can be used to interface other I2C modules with MPU6050
ADO	If more than one MPU6050 is used a single MCU, then this pin can be used to vary the address
Interrupt (INT)	Interrupt pin to indicate that

	data is available for MCU to read

Flex Sensor

Flex Sensors are only a variable resistor. The flex sensor obstruction changes when the sensor is twisted. They are generally accessible in two sizes 2.2 inches and 4.5 inches.

Why we use flex sensors in our task?

In this Gesture controlled Robotic Arm, a flex sensor

is utilized to control the gripper of the mechanical arm. At the point when the flex sensor on the hand glove is twisted, the servo engine joined to the gripper turns and the gripper opens.

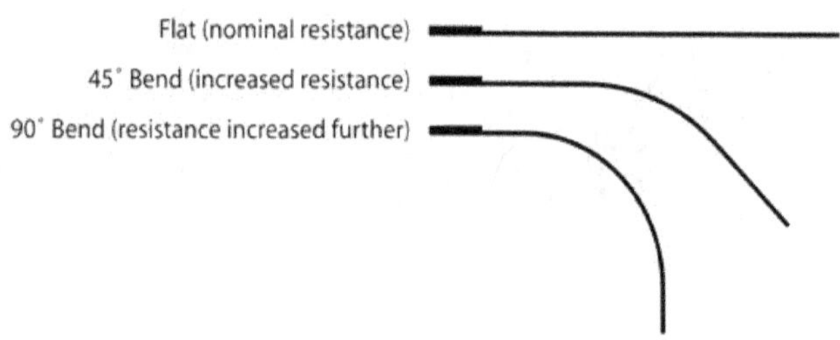

Flex sensors can be valuable in numerous applications and we have fabricated barely any undertakings utilizing Flex sensor like a game controller, Tone generator, along with etc.

Preparing the 3D printed Robotic ARM:

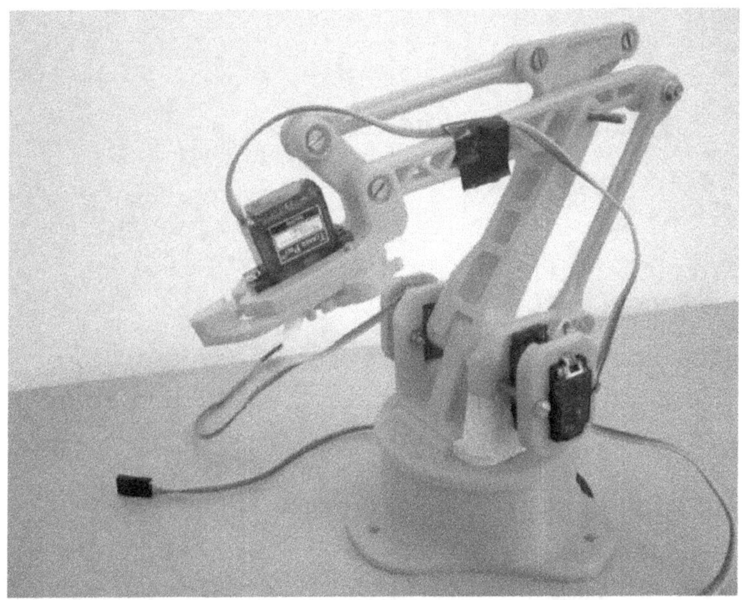

The 3D printed Robotic Arm utilized in this instructional exercise was made by following the structure given by EEZYbotARM which is accessible in the Thingiverse.

Above is the picture of my 3D printed Robotic Arm in the wake of collecting with 4 Servo Motors.

Parts Required:

- Arduino Nano

- Flex Sensor

- 10k Resistor

- MPU6050

- Hand Gloves

- Interfacing Wires

- Breadboard

Circuit Diagram:

The accompanying picture shows the circuit associations for Arduino based signal controlled Robotic Arm.

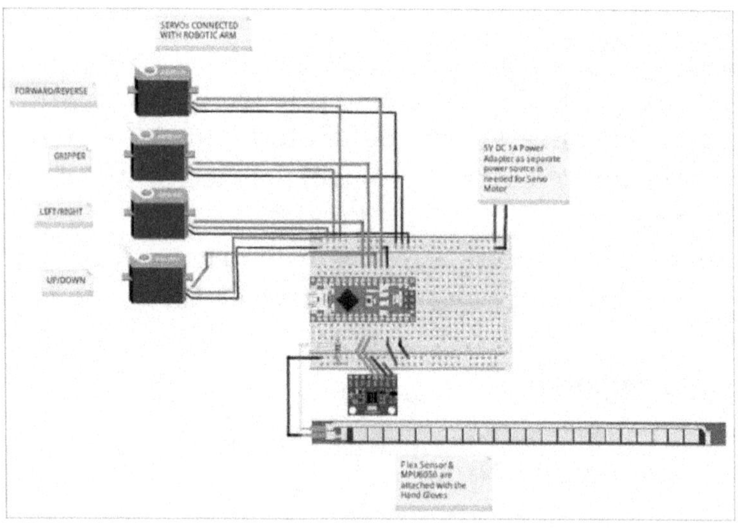

Circuit Connection between MPU6050 and Arduino Nano:

MPU6050	Arduino Nano
VCC	+5V
GND	GND
SDA	A4
SCL	A5

Circuit Connection between Servo Motors and Arduino Nano:

Arduino Nano	SERVO MOTOR	Power Adapter
D2	Servo 1 Orange (PWM Pin)	-
D3	Servo 2 Orange (PWM Pin)	-
D4	Servo 3 Orange (PWM Pin)	-
D5	Servo 4 Orange (PWM Pin)	-

GND	Servo 1,2,3,4 Brown (GND Pin)	GND
-	Servo 1,2,3,4 Red (+5V Pin)	+5V

A flex sensor contains two pins. It doesn't contain energized terminals. So the pin one P1 is associated with the Arduino Nano's Analog Pin A0 with a draw up resistor of 10k and the pin two P2 is grounded to Arduino.

Mounting MPU6050 and Flex Sensor to Gloves

We have mounted the MPU6050 and Flex Sensor onto a hand glove. Here a wired association is utilized to interface Glove and mechanical arm however it very well may be made remote by utilizing a RF association or a Bluetooth association.

After each association, the last arrangement for motion controlled Robotic Arm resembles the beneath picture:

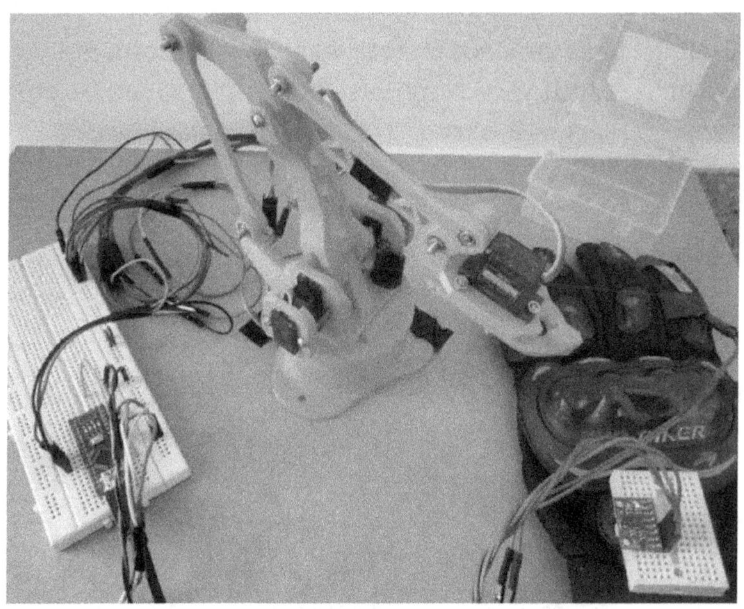

Programming Arduino Nano for Robotic Arm

Here a couple of significant lines of code are clarified.

1. In the first place, incorporate the fundamental library records. Wire.h library is utilized for I2C correspondence between Arduino Nano and MPU6050 and servo.h for controlling servo engine.

```
#include<Wire.h>

#include<Servo.h>
```

2. Next, the items for the class servo is announced. As we utilize four servo engines, four items, for example, servo_1, servo_2, servo_3, servo_4 are made.

```
Servo servo_1;

Servo servo_2;

Servo servo_3;

Servo servo_4;
```

3. Next, the I2C address of MPU6050 and the factors to be utilized is announced.

```
const int MPU_addr=0x68;        //MPU6050 I2C Address

int16_t axis_X,axis_Y,axis_Z;

int minVal=265;

int maxVal=402;

double x;
```

```
double y;

double z;
```

4. Next in the void arrangement, a baud pace of 9600 is set for Serial correspondence.

```
Serial.begin(9600);
```

Also, I2C correspondence between the Arduino Nano and MPU6050 is built up:

```
Wire.begin();               //Initilize I2C Communication

Wire.beginTransmission(MPU_addr);      //Start communication with MPU6050

Wire.write(0x6B);           //Writes to Register 6B

Wire.write(0);              //Writes 0 into 6B Register to Reset

Wire.endTransmission(true);           //Ends  I2C transmission
```

Additionally, four PWM pins are characterized for servo engine associations.

```
servo_1.attach(2);  // Forward/Reverse_Motor

servo_2.attach(3);  // Up/Down_Motor

servo_3.attach(4);  // Gripper_Motor

servo_4.attach(5);  // Left/Right_Motor
```

5. Next in the void circle work, again set up I2C association between the MPU6050 and Arduino Nano and afterward begin to peruse the X, Y, Z-Axis information from the register of MPU6050 and store them in relating factors.

```
Wire.beginTransmission(MPU_addr);

Wire.write(0x3B);               //Start with regsiter 0x3B

Wire.endTransmission(false);

Wire.requestFrom(MPU_addr,14,true);   //Read 14 Registers
```

```
axis_X=Wire.read()<<8|Wire.read();

axis_Y=Wire.read()<<8|Wire.read();

axis_Z=Wire.read()<<8|Wire.read();
```

From that point forward, map the min and max estimation of the hub information from the MPU6050 sensor in the scope of -90 to 90.

```
int xAng = map(axis_X,minVal,maxVal,-90,90);

int yAng = map(axis_Y,minVal, maxVal,-90,90);

int zAng = map(axis_Z,minVal, maxVal,-90,90);
```

At that point utilize the accompanying equation to compute the x, y, z esteems as far as 0 to 360.

```
x= RAD_TO_DEG*(atan2(-yAng, -zAng)+PI);

y= RAD_TO_DEG*(atan2(-xAng, -zAng)+PI);

z= RAD_TO_DEG * (atan2(-yAng, -
```

```
xAng)+PI);
```

At that point read the flex sensor Analog yield information at the Arduino Nano's A0 pin and as per the computerized estimation of the flex sensor set the servo edge of the gripper. So if the flex sensor information is more noteworthy than 750 the servo engine point of the gripper is 0 degree and if under 750 it is 180 degrees.

```
int gripper;

int flex_sensorip = analogRead(A0);

if(flex_sensorip > 750)

    {

        gripper = 0;

    }

    else

    {

        gripper = 180;
```

```
   }

servo_3.write(gripper);
```

At that point the development of MPU6050 on the X-hub from 0 to 60 is mapped as far as 0 to 90 degrees for the servo engine's Forward/Reverse movement the Robotic arm.

```
if(x >=0 && x <= 60)

{

  int mov1 = map(x,0,60,0,90);

  Serial.print("Movement in F/R = ");

  Serial.print(mov1);

  Serial.println((char)176);

  servo_1.write(mov1);

}
```

Furthermore, the development of MPU6050 on the X-hub from 250 to 360 is mapped as far as 0 to 90 degrees for the servo engine's UP/DOWN movement Robotic arm.

```
else if(x >=300 && x <= 360)

{

    int mov2 = map(x,360,250,0,90);

    Serial.print("Movement in Up/Down = ");

    Serial.print(mov2);

    Serial.println((char)176);

    servo_2.write(mov2);

}
```

Development of MPU6050 on the Y-pivot from 0 to 60 is mapped regarding 90 to 180 degrees for the servo engine's Left Movement of the Robotic arm.

```
if(y >=0 && y <= 60)

{

    int mov3 = map(y,0,60,90,180);
```

```
    Serial.print("Movement in Left = ");

    Serial.print(mov3);

    Serial.println((char)176);

    servo_4.write(mov3);

  }
```

Development of MPU 6050 in the Y-pivot from 300 to 360 is mapped regarding 0 to 90 degrees for the servo engine's Right Movement of the Robotic arm.

```
 else if(y >= 300 && y <= 360)

  {

    int mov3 = map(y,360,300,90,0);

    Serial.print("Movement in Right = ");

    Serial.print(mov3);

    Serial.println((char)176);

    servo_4.write(mov3);
```

```
}
```

Working of Gesture controlled Robotic Arm utilizing Arduino

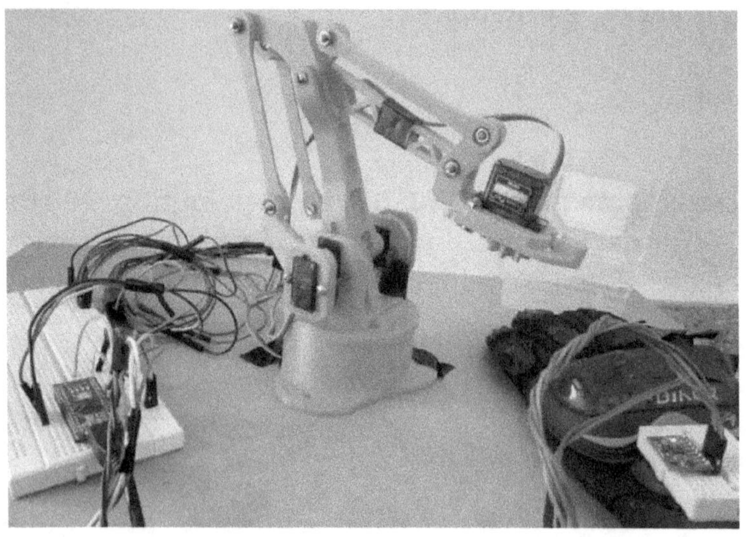

At long last, transfer the code to Arduino Nano and wear the hand glove mounted with the MPU6050 and Flex Sensor.

1. Presently move the hand down to push the automated arm ahead and climb to move the mechanical arm up.

2. At that point tilt the hand left or option to turn the mechanical arm left or right.

3. Curve the flex link joined with the hand glove's finger to open the gripper and afterward discharge it to close it.

Code

//Code for Gesture Controlled Robotic ARM (Arduino Nano & MPU6050)

```
#include<Wire.h>          //I2C Wire Library
#include<Servo.h>         //Servo Motor Library

Servo servo_1;
Servo servo_2;
Servo servo_3;
Servo servo_4;

const int MPU_addr=0x68;         //MPU6050 I2C Address
int16_t axis_X,axis_Y,axis_Z;
int minVal=265;
int maxVal=402;

double x;
double y;
double z;


void setup()
{
 Serial.begin(9600);
```

```
  Wire.begin();            //Initilize I2C Communication
  Wire.beginTransmission(MPU_addr);  //Start com-
munication with MPU6050
 Wire.write(0x6B);          //Writes to Register 6B
 Wire.write(0);            //Writes 0 into 6B Register to
Reset
 Wire.endTransmission(true);    //Ends I2C transmis-
sion


  servo_1.attach(2);  // Forward/Reverse_Motor
 servo_2.attach(3);  // Up/Down_Motor
 servo_3.attach(4);  // Gripper_Motor
 servo_4.attach(5);  // Left/Right_Motor


}

void loop()
{
 Wire.beginTransmission(MPU_addr);
 Wire.write(0x3B);          //Start with regsiter 0x3B
 Wire.endTransmission(false);
  Wire.requestFrom(MPU_addr,14,true);  //Read  14
Registers


  axis_X=Wire.read()<<8|Wire.read();        //Reads
the MPU6050 X,Y,Z AXIS Value
 axis_Y=Wire.read()<<8|Wire.read();
 axis_Z=Wire.read()<<8|Wire.read();
```

```
  int xAng = map(axis_X,minVal,maxVal,-90,90);    //
Maps axis values in terms of -90 to +90
  int yAng = map(axis_Y,minVal,maxVal,-90,90);
  int zAng = map(axis_Z,minVal,maxVal,-90,90);


  x = RAD_TO_DEG * (atan2(-yAng, -zAng)+PI);   //For-
mula to convert into degree
  y = RAD_TO_DEG * (atan2(-xAng, -zAng)+PI);
  z = RAD_TO_DEG * (atan2(-yAng, -xAng)+PI);

 int gripper;
 int flex_sensorip = analogRead(A0);        //Reads flex
sensor output


  if(flex_sensorip > 750)
    {
     gripper = 0;
    }
    else
    {
     gripper = 180;
    }


    servo_3.write(gripper);              //Writes gripper
value to 3rd servo motor


  if(x >=0 && x <= 60)
```

```
{
  int mov1 = map(x,0,60,0,90);
  Serial.print("Movement in F/R = ");
  Serial.print(mov1);
  Serial.println((char)176);
  servo_1.write(mov1);
}


  else if(x >=300 && x <= 360)
  {
   int mov2 = map(x,360,250,0,180);
   Serial.print("Movement in Up/Down = ");
   Serial.print(mov2);
   Serial.println((char)176);
   servo_2.write(mov2);
  }

if(y >=0 && y <= 60)
{
  int mov3 = map(y,0,60,90,180);
  Serial.print("Movement in Left = ");
  Serial.print(mov3);
  Serial.println((char)176);
  servo_4.write(mov3);
}


  else if(y >=300 && y <= 360)
  {
   int mov3 = map(y,360,300,90,0);
   Serial.print("Movement in Right = ");
```

```
    Serial.print(mov3);
    Serial.println((char)176);
    servo_4.write(mov3);
  }
}
```

THANK YOU